Teachi

M000303953

Some students find philosophy engrossing; others are merely bewildered.

How can professors meet the challenge of teaching introductory-level philosophy so that their students, regardless of initial incentive or skill, come to understand and even enjoy the subject?

For nearly a decade, renowned philosopher and teacher Steven M. Cahn offered doctoral candidates a fourteen-week, credit-bearing course to prepare them to teach undergraduates. At schools where these instructors were appointed, department chairs reported a dramatic increase in student interest. In this book, Cahn captures the essence of that course.

Yet many of the topics he discusses will concern all faculty, regardless of subject: a teacher's responsibilities, keys to effective instruction; the proper approach to term papers, examinations, and grades; and suggestions for how administrators should demonstrate that they take teaching seriously. Such matters are covered in the first seven chapters and the final, fourteenth chapter. The intermediate six chapters focus on teaching introductory philosophy and, in particular, on critical thinking, free will, philosophy of religion, ethics, and political philosophy.

Cahn's writing is lucid and lively, using vivid examples and avoiding educational jargon. In sum, this book is not only a guide on how to inspire students but also an inspiration for teachers themselves.

Steven M. Cahn is Professor Emeritus of Philosophy at the Graduate Center of The City University of New York. He is the author or editor of more than fifty books, including *From Student to Scholar* (2008); *Polishing Your Prose* (with Victor L. Cahn, 2013); *Happiness and Goodness* (with Christine Vitrano, 2015); and *Religion Within Reason* (2017).

STEVEN M. CAHN

Teaching
Philosophy
A Guide

Routledge
Taylor & Francis Group

NEW YORK AND LONDON

First published 2018
by Routledge
711 Third Avenue, New York, NY 10017

and by Routledge
2 Park Square, Milton Park, Abingdon, Oxon, OX14 4RN

Routledge is an imprint of the Taylor & Francis Group, an informa business

Library of Congress Cataloging-in-Publication Data
Names: Cahn, Steven M., author.
Title: Teaching philosophy : a guide / Steven M. Cahn.
Description: 1 [edition]. | New York : Routledge, 2018. | Includes
    bibliographical references.
Identifiers: LCCN 2017053088 | ISBN 9780815358558 (hardback) |
    ISBN 9780815358565 (pbk.)
Subjects: LCSH: Philosophy—Study and teaching.
Classification: LCC B52 .C325 2018 | DDC 107.1—dc23
LC record available at https://lccn.loc.gov/2017053088

ISBN: 978-0-8153-5855-8 (hbk)
ISBN: 978-0-8153-5856-5 (pbk)
ISBN: 978-1-351-12219-1 (ebk)

Typeset in Joanna MT and Din
by Apex CoVantage, LLC

With appreciation to
Maureen Eckert
Tziporah Kasachkoff
Peter Markie
David Shatz
Robert Talisse
Christine Vitrano

first my students, then my coauthors,
master teachers all

Contents

Acknowledgments

The impetus for this book came from a conversation with Robert Talisse, and I am grateful for his encouragement. Undoubtedly, my views on teaching philosophy have been influenced by my own teachers and colleagues. The former include Ernest Nagel, who originally encouraged me to pursue the study of philosophy, Justus Buchler, Arthur Danto, Charles Frankel, Sidney Morgenbesser, and especially my mentor, Richard Taylor. The latter include John O'Connor, James Rachels, Philip Kitcher, Patricia Kitcher, William Mann, George Sher, and David Rosenthal.

I am grateful to my editor Andrew Beck for his support and guidance, and to the staff at Routledge for assistance throughout production. My brother, Victor L. Cahn, Professor Emeritus of English at Skidmore College, himself a charismatic instructor, offered innumerable stylistic and substantive suggestions. My wife, Marilyn Ross, M.D., has helped in more ways than I can express in words.

Preface

When I am asked my vocation and reply that I teach philosophy, some people respond that philosophy was their favorite subject in college, while others moan that philosophy was the course they hated most. I attribute these reactions not to the subject but to those who taught it. Some succeeded; others failed. In either case, the attitudes they engendered have lasted a lifetime.

While I presume that readers of this book share my view that philosophy is engrossing, we should recognize that not all agree. Just as some individuals may have little initial taste for the study of German grammar, medieval music, or organic chemistry, so others have a similar lack of attraction toward philosophy. Yet they may be enrolled in courses for which we are responsible. Can we meet the challenge of teaching philosophy so that our students, regardless of initial interest, come to understand and even enjoy the subject?

If you don't care about the answer to this question, then, however strong your philosophical abilities, you're unlikely to succeed as a teacher. And those with the bad luck to be your students may well find that they have wasted their time, money, and energy.

Furthermore, our democratic society will lose an opportunity to provide some of its citizens with a key component of liberal education: the ability to scrutinize the fundamental principles of thought and action. The path to such intellectual perspective lies in the study of those subtle analyses and grand visions that comprise philosophy. No other subject affords a stronger defense against intimidation by dogmatism while simultaneously providing a framework for the operation of intelligence.

What can be done to avoid pedagogical failure? For nearly a decade I offered doctoral students in the Philosophy Program at the City University of New York Graduate Center a fourteen-week, credit-bearing course titled "Teaching Philosophy." The goal was to prepare new or inexperienced teachers to offer effective instruction for undergraduates. Through discussion of ethical obligations, preparation of sample syllabi and examinations, and numerous short teaching presentations by members of the class, dramatic results were achieved. Indeed, at the undergraduate institutions where the students went to teach, department chairs reported how well our students were performing and urged continued efforts to enhance the pedagogical skills of future instructors.

Sad to say, however, the majority of members in our doctoral program were focused entirely on increasing research productivity and believed time spent on improving teaching was wasted. Thus the course in teaching philosophy was abandoned, and as a result the undergraduate departmental chairs began to complain about our students' inadequate performance in the classroom.

On occasion, I have been asked whether I could capture in writing the essence of that course, so that its central insights might be widely available. Such is my attempt here. I recognize, of course, that no book can replace intensive practice with the guidance of a committed instructor and insightful comments from fellow students. Nevertheless, I hope that the suggestions I offer will prove useful.

I should add that here is not the place to score points in philosophical or meta-philosophical debates nor express support for any particular curricular or technological innovations. After all, teachers who excel in the classroom can hold varying intellectual positions, approach the subject in different ways, cover a variety of materials, and employ a range of pedagogical techniques. My focus is not on exploring such variations but on identifying and analyzing the fundamental elements of effective teaching.

In what follows I draw in part on my published books and articles. All the material, however, has been reworked to provide a unified presentation.

Here are my sources:

Cahn, Steven M., *The Eclipse of Excellence.* Public Affairs Press, 1973. Reprinted by Wipf and Stock Publishers, 2004.

—— *Education and the Democratic Ideal.* Nelson-Hall Company, 1979. Reprinted by Wipf and Stock Publishers, 2004.

—— *Saints and Scamps: Ethics in Academia.* Rowman & Littlefield, 1986. Revised Edition, 1994. 25th Anniversary Edition, 2011.

—— *Puzzles & Perplexities: Collected Essays.* Rowman & Littlefield, 2002. Second Edition, Lexington Books, 2007.

—— *From Student to Scholar: A Candid Guide to Becoming a Professor.* Columbia University Press, 2008.

One

A former colleague of mine once told me that her class in the history of modern philosophy was jumping from Leibniz to Kant, omitting the empiricists Locke, Berkeley, and Hume. When I asked why she was proceeding so oddly, she replied that she had asked her students to vote, and they had preferred not to study the empiricists.

The truth was that this instructor, knowing little about the empiricists, wanted to omit them but not be blamed for such an obvious gap. She tried to absolve herself of responsibility by describing the empiricists negatively, then asking her students their preference. She could have persuaded them of virtually anything, for, as far as they knew, Locke, Berkeley, and Hume might have been the outfield for the 1918 Boston Red Sox.

Teachers, however, cannot avoid responsibility for guiding the learning process. They should be expected to know which material is to be studied and in what order it is best presented. They should also understand how a student can proceed most productively, what constitutes individual progress, and when someone has achieved it.

Suppose you enroll in an introductory course in chess and your instructor begins by inquiring whether the class would prefer to learn first how rooks move or when castling is permitted. Such a question would be senseless, for a reasonable answer depends on some knowledge of chess, and if you already had that, you wouldn't be in a course for beginners.

As teachers are appropriately held responsible for what occurs in the classroom, so with responsibility goes authority. We speak not only of authority as power but also of *an* authority, that is, an expert. The two concepts are related, for the responsibilities that entail the exercise of authority or power are typically assigned to individuals by virtue of their presumed authority or expertise.

Such is the case with teachers, for their superior knowledge justifies their being assigned pedagogic responsibilities. After all, if teachers understand a subject no better than their students, why should students be charged tuition, while teachers receive paychecks? I have often heard teachers minimize their own importance and emphasize how much they learned from their students, but I have yet to hear a single professor offer to exchange an instructor's salary for a student's bill.

To recognize a teacher's authority, however, is not to suggest that the teacher should act in an authoritarian manner. The appropriate relationship is that of guide, not god.

Guides are expected to be familiar with the areas through which they lead, pointing out highlights and warning of dangers. They are to blame if you follow their instructions but miss important sites or fall victim to a peril that should have been anticipated. The guide who responds to charges of incompetence by blaming the visitors' lack of knowledge is not relieved of responsibility.

In this regard, college professors have something to learn from elementary school teachers. If second-graders fail to learn multiplication, the teacher cannot plausibly blame the students' weak mathematical talents; the problem obviously lies with the teacher. The same conclusion should be reached when a philosophy instructor reports that the students were unable to grasp why a valid argument might have false premises.

I remember an interview in which the candidate for a faculty position, when asked if he had any questions, inquired, "How strong are your students?" to which I responded, "How strong are the students at the school where you teach?" "So-so," he replied. "Then," I said, "you'll probably find ours to be the same." His query suggested that he focused more on the talents of students rather than on the quality of the instruction they receive, and I anticipated that his attitude toward his own students would be mirrored in his attitude toward ours.

Recognizing the extent to which students are necessarily dependent on their teachers leads to the realization of how much harm faculty members can inflict. Which of us has not felt the sting of an instructor's thoughtless or malicious gibe? Or been victimized by carelessness or meanness? Or developed a blindness or aversion to some potentially fascinating subject as a result of an incompetent, tedious, or aberrant presentation?

These reflections should lead to a realization implicit throughout this book: Teaching has an ethical dimension, for the teacher has the capacity to help or harm others. Achieving the former and avoiding the latter are the primary responsibilities of every instructor.

Two

Knowing a subject and knowing how to teach it effectively are quite different. No doubt you remember that during your own undergraduate and graduate careers you experienced much ineffective instruction. The problem was not primarily that the teachers were uninformed about the subject but that they did not know how to engage students. Information was presented, but the process was boring, confusing, or unsatisfying.

Yet some of your teachers found ways to lead students in grasping appropriate subject matter while arousing appreciation for it. Indeed, studying with a master teacher was likely a major reason you decided to pursue a career in philosophy.

Now the crucial question: What do successful teachers have in common that others lack? The answer is not a mysterious *je ne sais quoi* but attention to three strategic elements that lead to success.

1

The first is commonly referred to as "motivation." Without it, a class stagnates. After all, how long will you watch a movie that does nothing to capture your attention? Or read a novel that begins with a situation of no interest? The slower the start, the more difficult to generate enthusiasm. At best, the audience allows you a few minutes without much action. The same with teaching.

Consider the openings of the following two lectures, delivered as Presidential Addresses at the Eastern Division Meeting of the American Philosophical Association. Each talk was presented to an audience of approximately five hundred philosophers.

In 1970 the speaker was Wilfrid Sellars. His title was "this I or he or it (the thing) which thinks . . .", and he began as follows:

> The quotation which I have taken as my text occurs in the opening paragraphs of the Paralogisms of Pure Reason in which Kant undertakes a critique of what he calls 'Rational Psychology.' The paragraphs are common to the two editions of the *Critique of Pure Reason*, and the formulations they contain may be presumed to have continued to satisfy him— at least as introductory remarks.[1]

If you are a Kant scholar, you would probably be eager to read the rest of this talk, but if your interests lie elsewhere, you likely would prefer to move on.

You might suppose that Sellars's devoting his address to an exposition of a historical text unavoidably led much of his audience to lose interest, but that assumption would be mistaken. The proof is found in the address given a year earlier by Stuart Hampshire. He, too, expounded a historical text but offered a far more provocative opening. He began his talk, titled "A Kind of Materialism," as follows:

> I want to speak today about a philosophy of mind to which I will not at first assign an identity or date, except that its author could not have lived and worked before 1600. He is modern, in the sense that he thinks principally about the future applications of the physical sciences to the study of personality. As I speak, I hope that it will not at first be too easy for you to tell whether or not he is our contemporary,

whether indeed he is not present in this room. I attempt this
reconstruction as a way of praising a philosopher who has
not, I think, been at all justly interpreted so far.[2]

Hampshire's withholding the name of the author was a brilliant stroke, because members of the audience were immediately curious as to whom he was referring. Looking around, wondering if the subject was there, they treated Hampshire's every sentence as a clue. Finally, a few minutes from his conclusion, he revealed that the author in question was Spinoza, and Hampshire ended by quoting the passage from the *Ethics* that had been his unspoken focus: "The human mind not only perceives the affections of the human body, but also the idea of these affections" (I, 22).

Had Hampshire begun by quoting this text, the philosophical substance of his lecture would have been unchanged, but doing so would have been a pedagogical disaster, for few would have listened with special care. By making his talk a puzzle, however, Hampshire enthralled the audience, and having been present myself, I can testify that the quiet in the hall was striking.

Now let me ask: Do you admire Hampshire's strategy, or do you find it a distraction that could have been eliminated with no loss of philosophical content? If the latter, then whatever may be your skills as a philosopher, you're not thinking as a teacher, and your performance in the classroom is apt to leave your students uninterested and unresponsive. On the other hand, if you appreciate Hampshire's strategy, then I hope you will try to develop your own motivational devices that you can use each time you teach.

Walking into class and beginning, "Let's turn to page 179" will not generate electricity. If, though, you begin by presenting a challenging puzzle or stimulating thesis, your listeners are far more likely to become interested.

Here is an example that I offer not because of its profundity but simply because I found that it worked with students. (I should add that while my own success in the classroom does not match that achieved by some others I have known, I take second place to no one in my admiration for the performance of those I consider great teachers.) In teaching introductory philosophy, I usually include Mill's account of the case for free thought and discussion in Chapter Two of On Liberty. Although I assign the relevant pages for preparatory reading, I don't begin the class by referring to Mill or his book. Rather, I ask students to suppose that as they entered the building they saw a table where passersby were being urged to "sign the petition." Then I ask the students to imagine that they had strolled over to learn more and were invited to sign a letter, addressed to the administration, demanding that an invited speaker with a well-documented record of having expressed racist and sexist sentiments not be allowed to appear. I then ask the students whether they would sign the letter.

Most are sure they would, and the few holdouts quickly lose confidence in their position as others in the class accuse them of insensitivity to the feelings of those who are victims of prejudice. At that point I ask the question: Would John Stuart Mill sign the petition? Suddenly the students recognize the significance of Mill's defense of free expression in On Liberty, and they agree that Mill would refuse to sign. Then I ask students to explain Mill's view, and the discussion proceeds apace.

What such a motivational device does is make apparent the connections between seemingly esoteric material and the students' own sphere of experience, so that the subject itself becomes their personal concern. I know of no formula for developing effective motivational devices, which is one reason why teaching is an art, yet even a weak attempt to motivate is better than none.

Each time you enter a classroom you should have thought about how you plan to present the material so that students will become interested. You may not always find an effective means of achieving your goal, but when you do, you add to your repertoire of motivational techniques.

2

Even with a motivated student, though, a successful teacher needs to know how to take advantage of such interest. A key element is organization, presenting material in a sequence that promotes understanding.

To grasp the challenge, imagine trying to explain baseball to a person unfamiliar with the sport. Where would you begin? With the roles of the pitcher and catcher? How about the calling of balls and strikes? Or the location of the bases, how to score runs, or the ways outs can be made? The fundamental difficulty is that all these starting points presume knowledge of some of the others. How, then, can you break the circle of intertwining concepts and make the subject accessible?

Consider the following attempt: "In playing baseball you try to score runs. Only the team to whom the ball is pitched can score. You run around the bases and try to avoid outs. Four balls result in walks. The game has nine innings."

This attempt at teaching is a failure. Not that any of the statements is false. Each is true, yet not only disconnected from the previous ones but also presuming knowledge the listener doesn't possess.

The first statement refers to "runs," but the learner hasn't been told how a run is scored. The second statement refers to a ball being "pitched," but the role of the pitcher hasn't been explained. The remaining statements refer to "bases," "outs," "balls," "walks" and "innings," but none of these terms has been put in context. In short, if you don't already understand baseball, you won't learn much from this explanation. In other words, a presentation can be factual yet not pedagogically well organized.

Consider an experience common in the days before cars were equipped with GPS. You're driving through an unfamiliar town looking for the highway, and you ask directions from a passerby who responds, "It's easy. Just turn right at the supermarket, then turn left at the second light before the drugstore, then turn right at the stop sign near the post office, and you can't miss it." The problem is obvious. If you are a stranger in town and don't know where these landmarks are, how can you know when to make turns?

Let me next offer a philosophical example. Suppose you are planning to discuss Robert Nozick's concept of knowledge as tracking the truth. Unless you first explain the traditional three-part definition of knowledge, then ensure that everyone understands the challenge to that definition presented by the counterexamples associated with Edmund Gettier, trying to discuss Nozick's response to Gettier will leave the class in utter confusion. Even if your discussion of Nozick is insightful, if students are insufficiently prepared to grasp it, the pedagogical value will be lost.

Poor teachers may not care whether their students understand a presentation, but successful teachers are eager to explain basic points to those who have trouble with them. If someone has no interest in offering such help, that person is not cut out to be a teacher and is akin to a surgeon who is unhappy about having to deal with sick people.

The temptation is to argue that an explanation is successful if some students understand it. Effective teachers, however, direct their remarks not only at the best students, or at the top ten percent of the class, or even at the majority; instead, such teachers speak so that virtually all their listeners can follow. These teachers realize that when more than one or two students complain they are lost, many others, whether they themselves realize so, also need help.

Note that a concern for all students is compatible with caring about the progress of the best. After all, stronger students also benefit from a well-organized presentation, and their interest can be maintained with optional in-class challenges or extra-credit assignments. In truth, however, they need less, not more, help than others. Do you suppose Plato was especially worried whether he could keep Aristotle's attention? Stronger students deserve encouragement, but as they forge ahead on their own they may even challenge the instructor to keep up.

Is working with students who grasp material slowly less enjoyable than working with their more talented classmates? No doubt many teachers think so, but the point of teaching is not to bring enjoyment to teachers but to enlighten students. And although some are more difficult to reach than others, every student making an effort to learn should have the opportunity to do so. That aim can be achieved, however, only if material is presented in an effective order.

Years ago, I interviewed a candidate who was highly recommended for his pedagogical success. After listening to him present a rather convoluted talk, I doubted his reputation and asked him what percentage of the students in his introductory class understood his lectures. He replied proudly, "Definitely half." When I asked about the fate of the other half, he responded that they were not philosophically sophisticated enough to merit his attention. This attitude is not that of a good teacher. After all, every student, strong or weak, has paid tuition and deserves assistance in trying to succeed. And surely most have the necessary ability, assuming their instructor is capable and cares about reaching them.

In sum, just as you need to prepare a motivational strategy, so you need to plan the organization of your materials. Simply walking into the classroom and offering stream-of-consciousness instruction results in a class that meanders idly from one topic to another, as students lose their way.

Any subject can be rendered opaque if offered in a disorganized manner. Avoiding that result is a component of effective teaching.

3

Even a motivated and well-organized presentation, however, will be unsuccessful if not clear. And achieving clarity is no easy matter.

One problem is speaking too quickly. No matter what your content, if you speak too rapidly, you won't be understood. Indeed, the most obvious sign of a poor lecturer is rushing. When those who are inexperienced come to a podium, they hardly ever speak at a proper pace. With a genuine orator, however, sentences come slowly. No student will ever object to your speaking too deliberately, but many will complain if words cascade.

Another problem is using terms the audience doesn't understand. For example, early in my teaching career I was discussing with an introductory class John Hospers's article, "Free Will and Psychoanalysis," in which he refers to the "Oedipus complex." I assumed my students would understand this reference and failed to explain it. I soon realized my mistake, for not only was the Oedipus complex unfamiliar to them, but they had never heard of Oedipus. In such circumstances we tend to blame our students. Yet no matter how bright or well prepared they may be, they invariably do not know as much as we hope.

This guideline applies even to doctoral students. Five decades ago, when James Rachels and I were assistant professors at

New York University, we believed that our colleagues were assuming that the students were far better acquainted with the literature than, in fact, they were. Therefore as an experiment, we drew up a list of fifty famous books, most in the history of philosophy but a few in contemporary philosophy, and asked students to name the authors. The highest score any student achieved was in the thirties, most couldn't identify even half the books, and a few knew barely ten. Meanwhile, their professors acted as if the students were familiar with both the authors and contents of each of these books.

Thus a professor should not blithely assume that students understand such terms as rationalism, determinism, or emotivism. The rule should be: Don't introduce any term without explanation unless you would be willing to place a sizable bet that everyone in the class is familiar with it.

Another reason for lack of clarity is omitting steps in reasoning. Suppose an instructor offering an example of mathematical thinking says, "Given that $17 - 11 = 3x$, we all know that $2x = 4$." Some students in the class are sure to become lost because the teacher has failed to take the time to explain how the first equation proves that $x = 2$, hence $2 \times 2 = 4$.

But can't you omit what seems apparent? The question brings to my mind an incident, reported by a number of witnesses, involving W. V. O. Quine. While his textbook on symbolic logic was widely used, he didn't relish teaching the subject at the introductory level but was occasionally asked to do so. Once in such a course, after he wrote a proof on the board, a student raised his hand and asked impatiently, "Why bother writing out that proof? It's obvious." To which Quine replied, "Young man, this entire course is obvious." Clearly, what was obvious to Quine was not always obvious to others, just as what is obvious to a teacher may not be obvious to the students.

In sum, a successful teacher provides motivation, organization, and clarification. If students aren't motivated, don't see how matters hang together, or are confused by the presentation, then regardless of what the teacher may believe, the quality of instruction has fallen short.

Furthermore, these principles hold regardless of your philosophical orientation or your students' age, gender, race, ethnicity, religion, sexual orientation, economic status, or any other respects in which students can differ. Successful teachers are aware of whom they are teaching and adapt their methods to their audience. But in each case the fundamentals remain the same: motivate, organize, and clarify.

4

Even those who adhere to these principles may slip into various pedagogical pitfalls. These are more easily noticed by those who observe teachers rather than by the teachers themselves, but mentioning these traps may render them easier to avoid.

First, look at your audience, not at the chalkboard, the floor, the ceiling, or the window. Only by keeping your eyes on the students can you make contact with them and recognize when you have their attention.

Second, try to avoid verbal tics. Adding to every sentence "y' know," "right," "okay," or another such phrase distracts listeners and increases the difficulty of their concentrating on whatever you are trying to communicate.

Third, holding some object, such as a bottle of water or piece of chalk, and manipulating it endlessly as you speak diverts attention to the object rather than to what you're saying.

Fourth, use notes if necessary, but don't bury your head in them. Consult them occasionally if you prefer but don't read them at length, thereby losing connection with your audience.

Fifth, look around the room at all the students rather than concentrating your attention on a select few. Try to engage everyone, not just those who regularly volunteer. Remember that, when given the opportunity, those who are usually quiet may have much of value to contribute.

Sixth, don't ask questions without providing students with the opportunity to respond. And if the first answer to a question is unsatisfactory, encourage other students to react, rather than immediately answering the question yourself.

Seventh, nothing is amiss about admitting that you don't know the answer to a question and will try to find out for the next class session. After all, teachers, while knowledgeable, should not pretend to be omniscient.

Eighth, use examples whenever possible. Keep in mind, too, that the best ones are typically prepared ahead of time, when you can consider their appropriateness and effectiveness.

Ninth, be energetic. Passivity is not likely to create interest or excitement. Don't be surprised, however, if such exertion proves tiring. Effective teaching can be exhausting.

Tenth, students sometimes respond to your efforts to such a degree that they monopolize the classroom. I suggest calling them aside, explaining the problem, and urging them to assist you. I recall one instance in which a student in my class responded to every question I asked by immediately raising his hand and waving it wildly, thus distracting the other students. I called him to my office and urged him to give others a chance to participate. He protested, "But I know all the answers." I then suggested that we agree on the following plan. When I asked a question, I would look at him, and if he knew the answer he would not raise his hand but simply give a knowing nod. From then on he faithfully followed this new system and never again was a problem.

I can't claim that all the cases I had to deal with worked out as well. Sometimes nothing helps, and you may have to explain the situation to the head of your department and ask for assistance. Keep in mind, however, that difficulties are to be expected. After all, successful teaching is hard.

NOTES

1. Proceedings and Addresses of The American Philosophical Association, vol. XLIV (September, 1971), p. 5.
2. Proceedings and Addresses of The American Philosophical Association. vol. XLIII (September, 1970), p. 5.

Three

The terms "conscience," "conscious," and "conscientious" are related not only etymologically but also conceptually. A teacher with a conscience is conscious of pedagogical details and conscientious in ensuring that they are handled properly. Such a concern for detail is widely recognized as an element of first-rate scholarship, but should also be regarded as an element of first-rate teaching. While some may consider a discussion of mechanics to be petty, when these matters are neglected, students suffer the consequences.

To see this principle in practice, suppose you are asked to teach a particular course for the first time. How to proceed?

1

The initial step is to find out how the course is described in the department's curricular listing. That's the course the students are expecting to take, and thus the one you are supposed to teach. Perhaps later you'll write that description yourself, but until then you're bound by the announcement as posted.

Now comes a critical decision: Which materials will you ask students to read? The answer can be crucial to the success of the course.

One sign of a conscientious instructor is awareness of available texts. Those who lack that knowledge are apt to choose some articles with which they are familiar and make them available online. This strategy, however, raises problems. Only a relative small number of articles are chosen by the instructor, whereas a standard anthology may contain fifty to a hundred selections, plus introductions, study questions, bibliographies, a glossary, an index, and so on. Furthermore, whereas the items online reflect one instructor's view of the field, the anthology goes through a process in which the editors' judgment is reviewed by a dozen or more experts, then revised in light of the suggestions. When students study selections online, they are focusing only on what the instructor wants them to read; when they purchase an anthology, they receive an overview of the field and can peruse materials with which their instructor may even be unfamiliar. Granted, the price of a textbook can be prohibitive, which is a decisive reason not to use that volume, yet anthologies at reasonable price are usually available.

A further issue is the level of difficulty the book presents. In short, how hard are the readings? The same philosophical issue can be approached through either relatively simple selections or far more complex ones. The more demanding book may be an appropriate choice for a sophisticated audience, but assigning overly difficult readings to students unprepared to handle them is a common cause of pedagogical problems. Granted, studying philosophy is challenging, but why ask students to read what you know they cannot understand? The process makes no more sense than asking a beginning tennis player to try to return serves from a professional.

A common response from instructors who don't use a text is that none meets their needs. That claim, however, should be made only after all available options have been explored. Doing so takes considerable time and effort, yet students deserve no less.

2

The next step is to prepare a syllabus. This document is the student's guide to the course and should be presented at the first class meeting. It ought to indicate the assigned readings for each week, and while a change may be necessary, such alterations should be kept to a minimum. Otherwise, students become disoriented, and their plans for covering the material are upset.

How many pages should be assigned for each week? Enough to provide sufficient material for class discussion but not so much as to be overwhelming. If you don't have time in class to cover the readings, your list is too long. And if you don't believe a selection is worth discussion, then choosing it was probably a mistake.

The syllabus should also specify deadlines for any project, and they should be maintained. To treat those who are late the same as others is blatantly unfair, misleading to students, and self-defeating for instructors.

For instance, a professor of my acquaintance once stated a deadline for submission of term papers, then a week later announced that it had been extended for those who were having trouble, then another week later did the same again. Soon no one paid attention to any of these deadlines, and the professor spent the final days before commencement frantically grading a bushel of term papers so that students could graduate on time. The point is clear: Teachers who fail to show respect for their own rules do not deserve, and will not receive, the respect of others.

Some instructors append to the syllabus a bibliography, listing works that students can consult. Its value is in direct proportion to the quality of the annotation provided. A listing of hundreds of items with no commentary is bewildering and virtually useless. A student has time to consult only a few sources. Which are most important? What purposes might others serve? A bibliography that does not provide this essential information is hardly worth distributing.

Failure to provide a syllabus is a disservice to students, giving them no information as to the content of the course or its organization. The omission suggests a teacher's lack of planning or caring.

3

With a syllabus completed, are you ready for the first class? Not quite. Have you checked that the bookstore has your order on hand? If not, chaos may ensue when the students find that the books haven't arrived, or that those that have come are the wrong ones. Perhaps you requested J. L. Austin's *Sense and Sensibilia*, but the bookstore obtained Jane Austen's *Sense and Sensibility*. Simply checking can avoid weeks of confusion.

Visit the assigned room to make sure it fits your needs. If you're expecting fifty students and the room seats only thirty, you need to inform the registrar and have an appropriate change made. Or if you require video equipment but you don't know how to use the available resources, find out ahead of time and make such preparation as may be necessary. If the room is cavernous but your voice is not, perhaps a microphone can be arranged. Maybe the chairs are set in a way that hinders your approach. Or perhaps you have to decide where best to stand. (If possible, avoid a set-up where a clock is over your head, thus serving as a distraction.)

Remember that when politicians are scheduled to debate, they and their media staff come to the site ahead of time to check the setting, making sure it doesn't work against them. You should do the same. As environmental psychologists remind us, we are affected by the nature of the spaces we inhabit.

4

Now you are ready to plan the first day of the course. Do you need to do more than distribute the syllabus, then dismiss the class? Too many instructors squander the first session in just this way, only to complain at the end of the semester that they have run out of time. Any lost class, however, is a wasted opportunity, and students are entitled to the full complement of scheduled sessions.

On opening day, the instructor can set the tone by placing the subject in perspective, specifying requirements, and suggesting how students can most effectively approach their work. Here is the opportunity to explain what materials wil be covered as well as which aspects of the subject will not be explored. Should the students bring the textbook to class? How important is the assigned reading? Do you require attendance? (I don't, unless I am counting class participation in computing final grades.) Students anticipate the need to adjust to different teachers and styles, but you can help by being explicit about your approach.

An important issue for all is lateness. Teachers should begin class promptly and expect students to be present on time. An instructor who comes late encourages students to come late. Soon everyone is late, and the sessions are shortened. Students have paid for full class periods and deserve no less.

This point should be emphasized on the first day, as should the teacher's promise not to go beyond the scheduled end. Prolonging one class may cause lateness at the next, and students should not miss important material just because they have to leave. Beginning and ending on time is a principle that may seem elementary, but when systematically violated, can prove extraordinarily irritating.

A fundamental pedagogic obligation is being present at every meeting. If for reasons of the most serious moment teachers are forced to be absent, they should, if possible, arrange for qualified substitutes. Rescheduling should be a last resort, for invariably some students, because of a conflict, will lose their rightful opportunity to attend. Teachers who miss a class in order to go to a conference or participate in a symposium have wrongly chosen self-interest over professional obligation.

5

Faculty members should also be available to students for consultations. Office hours ought to be posted, and professors present as announced. Failing to appear, an all-too-common practice, is irresponsible. Not only do office hours benefit students, they also benefit the faculty, who should welcome the opportunity to talk to students and receive informal feedback. Incidentally, while exchanging e-mails with students may be educationally useful, doing so does not encourage the free-floating discussion more usually found in face-to-face visits.

If students are not coming to your office hours, the situation can be handled by announcing that you would like students to visit, that they needn't have a problem, but that you welcome the opportunity to chat. If this invitation is issued on several occasions, so as not to seem begrudging, students will appear, and teachers then can ask such questions as: "How's the course going for you," "How do you find the readings?" "Are you following the lectures," and so on. Reactions can prove revelatory.

Another seemingly simple, yet significant, benefit of office hours is that you meet students individually and more easily learn their names. I once asked a colleague about the progress of several of his students, and he turned out to be unaware they were in his class. His ignorance did not seem to bother him, despite the term's being half over and his enrollment only twelve. When you enter a store, restaurant, or medical office you visited previously, you are pleased when you are remembered. Students react similarly. Large classes make observing this principle difficult, but I have known a conscientious professor with classes of more than two hundred who cared enough to learn the name of every student and even some information about each. Such dedication is noticed and appreciated.

Four

In virtually every course, students are asked to complete specific assignments. An instructor should take whatever time is necessary to explain these in detail, making clear exactly what is expected. After all, if students do not understand what they are supposing to be doing, the fault is not necessarily theirs.

1

"Write a paper on some aspect of the course" is an irresponsible, vague direction, suggesting the professor has been either too lazy to think about suitable topics or too callous to care whether students become lost. Offering a choice of subjects is fine, but providing no guidance in choosing a project is apt to end badly. One of the hardest tasks for scholars is deciding which issues to pursue; asking beginning students to do likewise is impractical.

Should the paper be essentially a summary of other literature or a critical study of it? Does the paper depend on research in the library? If so, of what kind? How broad a topic is appropriate? How long should the paper be? Without answers to such questions, students are prone to confusion and dismay. Such ordinary problems are magnified in a philosophy course, where students may never have written a philosophy paper. Assuming they know how is unrealistic.

To avoid chaos, distribute specific instructions such as these:

In Book X of Plato's *Republic*, he refers to 'an ancient quarrel' between poetry and philosophy. Drawing on the dialogues we have studied, explain the reasons Plato offers for supposing such a quarrel exists. If you agree with Plato's views, explain why and indicate what you believe are the most promising possibilities for resolving the quarrel. If you do not agree, explain your replies to the strongest counterarguments Plato or others might offer. In preparing the paper, you need not consult any source outside the dialogues themselves. The paper should be approximately 2,000 words and is due March 6.

This assignment is demanding but not bewildering, and students who undertake it will be able to spend their time analyzing Plato's ideas, not guessing the intentions of their instructor.

In writing papers, students are prone to commit certain sorts of errors. Rather than waiting to correct these mistakes once they appear, why not anticipate the problems and alert students before they begin their work? Here are some suggestions that can be offered:

1. In explaining the views of others, be fair. Offering misleading versions of positions, then refuting them, is pointless.
2. When quoting, do so accurately. If words are placed in quotation marks, those words need to be exact. If changes are made, use ellipses to indicate omissions, and brackets to indicate additions.
3. Certain terms are so ambiguous that use of them without explanation is problematic. I would include "objective," "subjective," "natural," "absolute," "relative," "relevant," "diverse," "pragmatic," and "existential."

4. Anticipate objections to your position, explain them without distortion, then reply to them. The stronger the objections you consider and answer, the better your paper.
5. Quoting an authority rarely provides a satisfactory response to a criticism of your position. An explanation in your own words is usually needed.
6. Proofread your paper to avoid misspellings and typographical errors.
7. Writing clearly is a virtue. Try to avoid wordiness and confusion.

Each instructor can add to this list, but the idea is to anticipate mistakes, not wait for them to occur and then criticize them.

Papers should be returned with detailed comments. For a student to prepare material carefully, then receive only a brief note such as "C: good try" is disheartening. Students are entitled to be informed which aspects of their work are well done and which unsatisfactory, as well as how future efforts might be enhanced.

Providing the chance for improvement is reason to assign several short papers rather than a single long one. Apart from the difficulty of writing an extended piece of philosophical work, shorter papers afford the opportunity to learn from reactions to earlier efforts and perform better on later ones.

A related concern is that papers be handed back to students within a short time. Otherwise, in preparing future assignments the students will be unable to utilize the instructor's suggestions, and may even stop caring about the whole matter. Sometimes outside a professor's office is a box of papers, submitted months before and eventually corrected by the instructor, but never retrieved by those who wrote them. This sad sight is evidence of professorial negligence and student alienation.

2

Papers, however, are not the only tool for assessing achievement. Another is examinations, whose purpose is to evaluate the scope and depth of a student's knowledge. Just as athletes are tested under game conditions and musicians under concert conditions, so students are tested under examination conditions to reveal whether they are in control of essential material or possess only a tenuous grasp of it. To speak glibly about a subject is not nearly as indicative of one's knowledge as to reply without prompting to pertinent questions and commit those answers to paper so they can be scrutinized.

Granted, examinations don't challenge students in the same way as papers do, but then papers don't challenge students as exams do. Writing papers calls for the ability to present a sustained piece of philosophical thinking, a task that demands more time than is usually available for an examination. Yet rarely do papers require mastery of most or even much of the course material. Moreover, in writing papers students can receive help outside the classroom from sources unavailable within. For those reasons, almost all students, given the choice, opt for a paper rather than an exam. That option, however, is not always appropriate.

Examinations, to be sure, are not the best test of imaginative power, but to suppose that original thinking flows from those uninformed about relevant fundamentals is unrealistic. Mastery of a field requires control of basic information and skills. These are the focus of effective exams.

Constructing them, however, requires care. To begin with, they should be representative of the course material. If a basic course in ethics covers Aristotle, Kant, and Mill, then the final should require knowledge of all three, not only the one the student prefers. Furthermore, the questions should not be repetitive, so that missing one answer interferes with replying to several others. The questions should also avoid ambiguity, which is why showing the exam to a colleague ahead of time can prove useful.

Whether students should be asked to write essays or reply to a series of shorter questions is a matter of preference. If longer answers are preferred, then avoid a formless query such as, "Does anything in the work of Descartes help us understand ourselves?" Instead, try a sharply focused, significant question such as, "Both Descartes and Berkeley raise doubts about the existence of the material world. Compare and contrast the arguments they use to raise these doubts and their conclusions as to whether their doubts can be resolved." Answering requires mastery of the subject, not merely the memorization of trifles or the improvisation of hazy, high-flown vacuities.

My own preference, however, is for an exam to consist of a series of short, pointed questions requiring no more than a paragraph to answer and calling for responses that are demonstrably right or wrong. Here, for example, are three items out of twelve I presented on a test for my students in an introductory course:

1. "If what you say is false, then anything implied by what you say is also false." Is that claim correct? If so, why? If not, why not?
2. In what way does hard determinism differ from soft determinism?
3. According to James Rachels, is a concern for one's own welfare incompatible with a genuine concern for the welfare of others?

These questions are intended to demonstrate whether students have a firm grasp of essentials or don't understand key points.

A distinct advantage of such a test is that it can be graded quickly, assigning each reply a 1 for a correct answer, 1/2 for a partially correct answer, or 0 for an incorrect answer, then summing the numbers and assigning a letter grade based on a reasonable scale. The teacher can also easily review the test in class, indicating to students the correct answers as well as the pages where they can be found. Little room remains for debate, and students can see clearly whether they are learning effectively.

While structuring an exam in this way works well for courses in introductory philosophy or introductory ethics, especially those with large enrollments, I have even used the system in a graduate course in the history of political philosophy, an educational level where examinations are rarely employed. Yet I adopted that approach because I wanted my students to do the readings assiduously, mastering the details of central texts by Plato, Aristotle, Hobbes, Locke, Rousseau, Hume, Madison, Marx, Mill, Rawls, and Nozick, as well as The Declaration of Independence and The Constitution of the United States. Had I simply asked students to write a term paper, they probably would have concentrated on a single topic, such as Rousseau's idea of the general will or Locke's theory of property, while not bothering to do much of the rest of the reading. In that case they wouldn't even realize how little they knew about the subject.

Instead, I constructed a ten-question mid-term for students to assess their progress (not counted unless they did well) and then a cumulative two-hour final with twenty-five items along these lines:

1. "The individual is prior in nature to the city." Does Aristotle agree? Why?
2. According to Hobbes, do the laws of nature oblige in foro externo? Why?
3. According to Rousseau, can a person be forced to be free? Why?

I even added a short section of quotations to be identified by author, such as "Man is born free, and everywhere he is in chains." Or: "Prudence, indeed, will dictate that governments long established should not be changed for light and transient causes; and accordingly all experience has shown that mankind are more disposed to suffer, while evils are sufferable, than to right themselves by abolishing the forms to which they are accustomed." Some students assume the former statement is by Marx, but those with a firmer grasp of the material recognize it as found near the beginning of Rousseau's *Of the Social Contract.* The longer statement is presumed by many to be authored by Locke, but it comes from the second paragraph of *The Declaration of Independence.* Weak students will miss almost every quotation, stronger ones will identify many, and only the most knowledgeable will recognize all the passages.

Such a test might appear to be focused excessively on details, but the result of presenting this challenge was that students concentrated their efforts on reading with care, listening attentively in class as I reviewed key points of each author, and even (to my surprise) voluntarily forming study groups to prepare for the exams, quizzing one another to gain mastery of these crucial works. Later, they reported how much they had learned and how pleased they were to have such a firm grasp of the fundamental texts of political philosophy.

I should note, though, that, to serve their appropriate purpose, examinations at any level should not be too long. Students working at a normal pace should have time to read the questions carefully, think about them, write legible answers, and reread them. Otherwise, the exam turns into a race and loses its value. Most students should be able to hand in their papers slightly ahead of the finish.

Another pitfall is the omission of clear directions. Imagine sitting down to begin work and reading the following instructions: "Answer three questions from Part I and two questions from Part II, but do not answer questions 2, 3, or 5 unless you also answer questions 8 and 9." By the time students have understood these rules, they will already be short of time and, understandably tense, may bungle the proceedings. An exam should be a test of knowledge and skills, not of the ability to solve verbal puzzles.

An additional problem is neglecting to announce the relative importance of each answer in grading the test. Suppose students are required to undertake three questions but are not told that the instructor considers the third more important than the other two combined. Students may spend equal time on each, never realizing they should concentrate time and effort on the last. Their mistake would indicate no lack of knowledge but be a result of the secret scoring system. Fairness implies that students realize how much each item is worth, so they can plan their work accordingly.

One helpful grading technique is evaluating each paper without knowing its author. An answer from a regularly good student may seem more impressive then the same response from a usually poor one. Also advisable is not grading tests by reading them from start to finish, but instead judging all answers to one question at a time. Teachers will thus pay close attention throughout rather than skimming after perusing only one or two responses. Furthermore, correcting exams this way lessens the possibility that the instructor will alter standards, because stabilizing them for various answers to the same question is far easier than doing so for entire tests.

As with papers, examinations should be graded with comments and returned promptly, ideally at the next class meeting. Students eagerly await the outcome, and especially if they have not done well, need to become aware as soon as possible of their problems. Faculty members who procrastinate, whether from laziness or indifference, and return exams after many weeks are doing a disservice to their students.

In some courses, examinations might be out of place, whereas in others, such as elementary logic, they are the most appropriate means of assessment. In short, they are only one tool of evaluation, but their usefulness should not be overlooked.

Five

Many teachers are uncomfortable with grades, viewing them as inherently inaccurate devices that in attempting to measure people, only traumatize and dehumanize them. This concern, however, is a tangle of misconceptions.

A grade represents an expert's judgment of the quality of a student's work in a specific course. As such, the mark not only indicates whether students are making satisfactory progress or earning academic honors, but also aids students in judging past efforts and formulating future plans.

Would these functions be better served if, as some have suggested, grades were replaced by letters of evaluation? In addition to the impracticality of a professor's writing hundreds of individual comments and evaluators reading thousands, the value of such letters would be severely limited if they didn't include specific indications of students' levels of performance, in other words, grades. Otherwise, the letters would be more likely to reveal the teachers' literary styles than the students' academic accomplishments. Remarks one instructor considers high praise may be used indiscriminately by another, whereas comments intended as mild commendation might be mistaken as tempered criticism.

While a piece of work would not necessarily be graded identically by all specialists, members of the same department usually agree whether a student's performance has been outstanding, good, fair, poor, or unsatisfactory, the levels of achievement typically symbolized by A through F. Granted, experts sometimes disagree, but in doing so they do not obliterate the distinction between their knowledgeable judgments and a novice's uninformed impressions.

What of the oft-repeated charge that grades are impersonal devices that reduce people to letters of the alphabet? That criticism is misguided. A grade is not a measure of a person but of a person's level of achievement in a particular course. The student who receives a C in introductory philosophy is not a C person with a C personality or C moral character but one whose performance in introductory philosophy was acceptable but in no way distinguished. Perhaps the student will do much better in later courses and even excel at philosophy, but this first try was not highly successful.

Whether grades are fair, however, depends on a teacher's conscientiousness in assigning them. One potential misuse is to award grades on bases other than a student's level of achievement. Irrelevant criteria include a student's gender, race, nationality, physical appearance, dress, personality, attitudes, innate capacities, and previous academic record. None of these factors should even be considered in deciding a student's grade. Performance in the course should be the only criterion.

If an A in symbolic logic might mean that the student tried hard, came from a impoverished community, or displayed an ingratiating personality, then the A is hopelessly ambiguous and serves no purpose. If, on the other hand, the grade signifies that the student had a firm grasp of the essentials of symbolic logic, then the message is clear.

The most effective means for assuring that no extraneous factors will enter into grading is for the instructor to make clear at the beginning of the term how final grades will be determined. How much will the final examination count?

How about the papers and other short assignments? Will a student's participation be a factor? Answering these questions at the outset enables students to concentrate their energies on the most important aspects of the course, not waste time speculating about the instructor's intentions.

Yet if the announced system is unnecessarily complicated, it can distort the purpose of the course. For example, if the teacher announces that to receive an A you need to accumulate 950 points out of 1000, and the final exam is worth 350, each of the other two exams is worth 120, each of the two papers is worth 140, and class discussion is worth 130, the class has taken on the elements of a complicated game show. The rule of thumb is: Explain your grading system, but keep matters simple.

The most common misuse of the grading system is the practice commonly referred to as "grading on a curve." The essence of this scheme is for the instructor to decide before the course begins what percentage of students will receive each grade. This method may produce aesthetically pleasing designs on a graph but is nevertheless conceptually confused. While a student's achievement should be judged in the light of reasonable expectations, these do not depend on such haphazard circumstances as the mix of students who happen to be taking the course simultaneously.

Consider the plight of a student who earns an eighty on an examination but receive a D, because most classmates scored higher. Yet the following semester in the same course, another earns an eighty with the same answers and receives an A, because this time almost all classmates scored lower. Two students, identical work, different grades: the system is patently unfair.

Years ago I overheard a student complain to the instructor about receiving a B. This nationally known scholar responded sympathetically but explained with regret that all the As were gone. His philosophical skills far exceeded his pedagogic wisdom.

Why do too many instructors resort to this approach? Because by doing so they avoid responsibility for determining the level of work each grade represents. They are also free to construct examinations without concern for skewed results, because even if the highest grade is thirty out of one hundred, grading on a curve will yield apparently acceptable consequences. Yet the appearance is deceiving, because rank in class will have been confused with mastery of subject. The Procrustean practice of grading on a curve rests on this muddle and should be abandoned (although inept teaching or badly constructed examinations should not be allowed to yield unconscionably low grades).

A different distortion of the grading system, rare nowadays, is an unwillingness to award high grades. Instructors who adopt this attitude take pride in rigor. But just as a third-grade student who receives an A in mathematics need not be the equal of Isaac Newton, so a freshman may deserve an A without being the philosophical peer of Aristotle. Receiving an A in an introductory course does not signify that a student has mastered philosophy, only that, considering what can reasonably be expected, the individual has done excellent work. A teacher who rarely awards high grades is failing to distinguish good from poor work. Doing so does not uphold academic standards but only misinterprets the grading symbols, thereby undermining their appropriate functions.

A more common misuse is the reluctance to award low grades, a practice popularly known as "grade inflation." It results from the unwillingness of professors to give students the bad news that they have not done as well as they might have hoped. Yet maintaining academic standards rests on the willingness of instructors to tell the truth. Understandably, some are concerned about the possible injustice of giving their own students realistic grades while other students receive inflated ones. The solution, adopted at some colleges, is for transcripts to include not only a course grade but also the average grade in the course. In this way grade inflation is publicly exposed, and unfairness dissipated. In any case, each inflated grade adds to the problem.

Yet awarding grades also calls for a sense of fair play. Consider a professor I knew who gave relatively easy exams throughout the semester, thereby leading students to believe they were doing well. The final examination, however, was vastly more difficult, and many students were shocked and angered to receive low grades for the course. Clearly this instructor misled and harmed his students. He was like a storeowner who announces a major sale but applies low prices only to a few rarely sought items.

After all, ethics applies not only to physicians, nurses, lawyers, business managers, journalists, and engineers but also to teachers. They, too, can lie, mislead, and fail to fulfill all manner of professional responsibilities. Indeed, classrooms are no more free of misconduct than hospitals, courts, or boardrooms.

Grading is especially sensitive to mishandling, because assessments are done in private, and results are not easily challenged. Instructors, therefore, need to be aware of this pitfall, and make every effort to treat students equitably.

Six

As I mentioned at the outset, teachers may lead students to find lifetime fulfillment, or inflict an aversion to learning that is never overcome. Granted, the effects of taking a single course may be minimal, but even so instructors may never realize the impact of what they have said and done.

One temptation professors need to resist is to allow their pedagogical authority to lead them into talking and acting as if their judgments are beyond reproach. Remember that faculty members typically hold sway without the threat of serious intellectual challenge. They comprehend complexities that lie beyond the understanding of a class and therefore can easily become enamored of their own erudition. Yet professors can be ignorant about many fields of endeavor, even including aspects of their own subject. They should never suggest otherwise.

Indeed, whenever a faculty member states opinions not shared by other reputable scholars, students ought to be so informed. They are entitled to know whether their teacher is expressing a consensus or only a majority or minority viewpoint. For an instructor to defend personal beliefs is appropriate, but serious alternatives should not be neglected. A faculty member should always keep in mind this question: If another qualified instructor were in my place, might that individual offer opinions that differ from my own? If so, the teacher should alert students and thereby contribute to their understanding.

For example, when teaching introductory philosophy, I discuss the problem of free will and determinism (about which more later). Although I believe the two are incompatible, I recognize that my view is a minority one, hence I do my best to explain as persuasively as possible the arguments that have been offered by those with whom I disagree. I hope that were they in the room, they would agree that I had not distorted their position.

After all, if you are unable to make a case against your own stance, then you don't know the issue well enough to teach it effectively. For that reason, one of my favorite strategies in oral exams is to ask candidates their position on an issue, then invite them to explain the best arguments against their view. Only those with a thorough understanding of the matter can answer effectively. As John Stuart Mill writes, "He who knows only his own side of the case knows little of that."[1]

For instance, I like to ask defenders of materialism to explain the strongest arguments for dualism, defenders of democracy to explain the strongest arguments for aristocracy, or defenders of abortion rights to explain the strongest arguments for a right to life. Such tasks are challenging, and success is clear evidence of mastery.

On the other hand, students should not be led to suppose that all expressed opinions are equally viable. Some arguments are valid, others invalid. Some hypotheses are well-founded, others not. A claim may be self-contradictory, run counter to the available evidence, be unclear, or mean nothing at all. Open-mindedness does not require obliterating the differences between clarity and obscurity, accuracy and carelessness, knowledge and ignorance. Instructors should be willing to insist on these distinctions.

Overlooking them due to concern about the possible effects of criticism on a student's psyche misunderstands the professor's role. Granted, some students are emotionally unstable. But in those cases we need to remember that a philosopher is not a clinical psychologist. Students dealing with a personal difficulty should be advised to visit the school's counseling service rather than be treated by a medical tyro, however well-meaning.

One issue about the proper relationship between instructor and student demands special attention, having been the source of some of the most egregious instances of professorial malfeasance. I refer to the view that teachers ought to be friends with their students. What is wrong with this approach, Sidney Hook points out, is that teachers "must be friendly without becoming a friend, although [they] may pave the way for later friendship, for friendship is a mark of preference and expresses itself in indulgence, favors, and distinctions that unconsciously find an invidious form."[2] Faculty members ought to care abut the progress of each student, but they should remain dispassionate, able to deliberate, judge, and act without thought of personal interest or advantage. Even the appearance of partiality is likely to impair the learning process by damaging an instructor's credibility, causing students to doubt that standards are being applied fairly.

Thus every teacher should be scrupulous in ensuring that no student receives preferential treatment. If one is permitted to write a paper instead of taking an examination, that option should be available to everyone in the class. If one is allowed to turn in an assignment late, then all others in similar circumstances should be offered the same opportunity. And if one is invited to the professor's home for dinner, then everyone should receive invitations. Adherence to this rule never leads to trouble; breaking it is often problematic.

One obvious implication of the principle of equal consideration is that between teacher and student not only is friendship inappropriate but even more so is romance. Even if a student never enrolls in a professor's classes, their liaison suggests that this faculty member does not view students from a professional standpoint. If an attempt is made to keep the relationship secret, the professor's integrity is compromised. In any case, such efforts at concealment almost always fail, thus besmirching the professor's reputation for honesty.

If a student seeks to initiate an affair with a professor, the only proper response is an unequivocal refusal. On the other hand, for a professor to attempt to seduce or coerce a student is an egregious abuse of authority that provides strong grounds for dismissal.

When a student has left the college or moved to a different unit of the university, whatever personal contact may develop with a professor is up to the two of them. During the years of undergraduate or graduate study, however, the only appropriate relationship is professional. To maintain these bounds is in everyone's best interest, and no more so than in the context of scholarly collaboration.

For whatever reasons, philosophers have recently had more than their share of scandals involving forms of sexual harassment or abuse. Under these unfortunate circumstances, those who teach philosophy should be especially vigilant to maintain their proper function as guides through a field of study. They should not seek or accept the role of psychiatrist, friend, or lover.

NOTES

1. John Stuart Mill, On Liberty (Lanham, MD: Rowman & Littlefield, 2005), p. 64.
2. Sidney Hook, Education for Modern Man: A New Perspective (New York: Alfred A. Knopf, 1963), pp. 230–231.

Seven

While my emphasis in this work is primarily on teaching undergraduates (a subject I'll return to shortly), we should not overlook pedagogical issues that arise in doctoral education. There the quality of instruction is frequently disappointing.

1

The source of the problem is that professors too often presume that by teaching at an advanced level they have transcended the need to observe principles of good pedagogy. Thus motivation may be omitted as unnecessary, organization denigrated as prosaic, and clarification spurned as simplistic. No wonder graduate students find many of their classes dreary or bewildering.

Unfortunately, professors are tempted to consider any doctoral course, even a first-level one, primarily as an opportunity to develop their own research and enlist supporters in the effort to work on its fine points. For instance, an instructor may decide to distribute chapters of the instructor's own forthcoming book and ask students to help edit the manuscript. Such an approach may provide insights into recent scholarship, but the question that doesn't even arise is whether this procedure is the best way to promote a thorough and balanced understanding of a discipline's fundamental methods and materials. As a result, doctoral students may also be led to suppose that their professors' opinions dominate the field, only to find later that competing views are at least as influential.

This egocentric style of graduate teaching is also flawed in suggesting to students that professional success depends on sharing their instructors' intellectual outlooks. Professors should not attempt to attract devoted bands of personal disciples; that goal is appropriate for gurus. Graduate faculty members should hope to foster a future generation of well-informed, independent-minded scholars, and courses should be conducted to achieve that aim.

A most unfortunate side effect of much graduate teaching is conveying the message that ignorance is ignominious. If students admit that they are unfamiliar with a particular author, work, concept, or position, they risk ridicule. Thus to maintain their dignity, even when confused they are encouraged to feign understanding. Instead of confessing, "I'm unfamiliar with that philosopher," "I don't know the book you cited," or "I'm not following the argument you presented." they nod as if comprehending every word. In short, contra Socrates, the goal is always to appear knowledgeable.

The opposite, however, ought to be the case. Professors should encourage students to indicate when they are lost. Such admissions should be met not with a put-down but with a compliment for intellectual honesty. After all, those afraid to admit what they do not know are defenseless against others who indulge in obfuscation.

These days, signs around the country tell us that if we see something, we should say something. Graduate students should be urged to follow an analogous rule: If you don't understand something, say something.

2

The most critical area of a graduate professor's responsibility is advising students on their doctoral dissertations, and here horror stories are legion. These include the typical tale of the advisor who suggests a subject so difficult that it would take decades to complete; or who does not return a student's work for many months; or who, without making clear exactly what the problems are, insists that drafts be endlessly revised. Students subjected to such treatment can become so filled with frustration, resentment, and anger that they find continuing their work impossible.

Advisors should help, not hinder, progress. While guiding outstanding advisees is a delight, not all advisees will excel. Yet with assistance most can complete the task at hand in a manner that is acceptable. The aim is to help them do so, not make their lives miserable by criticizing them for failing to attain levels of achievement beyond their reach.

A common problem is lack of a suitable topic. Typically students want to tackle one of vast magnitude, thereby making completion a virtual impossibility. The effective advisor is aware of this tendency and offers alternatives that are far easier to manage. After all, when a Ph.D. is awarded, the diploma doesn't indicate the scope of the dissertation or how long a student labored to complete it. The idea is to finish and move on to a career. Pet projects do not always make suitable dissertations.

My experience has been that the undertaking should take twelve to eighteen months; any time beyond two years is excessive. An effective advisor encourages students to finish in that time frame and enables them to do so. Drafts should be returned promptly, criticisms should be constructive rather than destructive, and the process should be demanding, not demoralizing. Indeed, in some cases completing the dissertation may be a highlight of doctoral education, and the reason typically is the positive attitude engendered by working with a supportive advisor.

3

Dissertation supervisors are expected to write letters for their advisees as they seek an academic position. But what if their work has been no more than satisfactory? In that case, a candid letter might doom the advisee's prospects.

How to proceed in such circumstances? George Sher suggests:

> To do what we can for our weaker students, we can try to write letters that will not disqualify them outright and that may be overlooked if their other letters come in stronger, while to preserve at least a tenuous connection to the truth, we can avoid saying things that are flatly false while playing up every scrap of positive information that is even marginally relevant.[1]

His advice accurately captures common practice, but is it justifiable? I believe so, but to avoid misunderstanding we need to distinguish two types of evaluations: assessments and recommendations. An assessment is written about someone with whom you have no personal relationship (or are not supposed to be influenced by any) and is expected to be a forthright judgment of the individual's merits. If, for example, you are asked whether someone is qualified to be granted tenure, you should provide a full account of the individual's strengths and weaknesses as you see them. If, in your view, the individual does not merit tenure, you should say so without fudging.

A letter of recommendation, however, is understood by all to be written in support of a candidate. You are expected to make the best case you can, while avoiding misrepresentation. After all, if you are identified as the candidate's advisor or dissertation committee member, you are expected to present a positive picture rather than dwell on a candidate's weaknesses.

In brief, when you are asked to provide an evaluation, be sure to understand whether you are being asked for an assessment or a recommendation. Then proceed accordingly. Failure to follow this guideline results in the sort of remark I once saw in a letter of recommendation from a faculty member who wrote, "Arthur [a pseudonym] is not among the best students I have taught, but he is not among the worst either." Although the writer actually thought rather well of Arthur and had been more than willing to write in his behalf, that remark doomed Arthur's chances for a faculty position. The writer had confused a recommendation with an evaluation, thereby stating what was true yet inappropriate.

NOTE

1. George Sher, "Global Norming: An Inconvenient Truth," in Robert B. Talisse and Maureen Eckert, eds., *A Teacher's Life: Essays for Steven M. Cahn* (Lanham, MD: Lexington Books, 2009), p. 110.

Eight

Shifting our attention from graduate students to beginners, we turn to challenges faced in teaching introductory philosophy courses. These are typically structured in one of four ways. Each has its advantages and disadvantages. Which to choose depends on many factors, including the instructor's style of philosophy and the background of the students, but any approach can be well or poorly done.

1

When I taught at Vassar College in the mid-1960s, every student who wished to take philosophy was required to begin with a two-semester sequence in the history of the subject. The first concentrated on Plato and Aristotle, as well as their immediate predecessors and successors, while the second focused on Descartes, Spinoza, Leibniz, Locke, Berkeley, Hume, and Kant. Virtually every member of the department taught this demanding course. Although to be fully prepared most instructors had to put in extra work, all students obtained a thorough foundation. Furthermore, teachers in every subsequent philosophy class could rely on all their students' possessing knowledge of the history of philosophy.

Taught in this way, introductory philosophy provides historical perspective, and students are apt to be excited by the array of great books and ideas. Ancient and modern philosophy are given their due, and students read in chronological order many works that have strongly influenced the development of Western thought.

Not surprisingly, students are more easily motivated to read a classic text by a renowned thinker rather than an article by a recent scholar unknown to them. Further, most great works of the past, unlike contemporary journal articles, were not intended only for specialists. They embody a breadth of vision that has inspired generations, and reading at least some of these works in their entirety is intellectually fulfilling.

This approach, however, also has its disadvantages. It suggests that philosophy is mainly the contemplation of works written long ago, and students may be led to suppose that their sole obligation is to grasp what others have said, not to think critically. This problem is magnified by the need to spend much time and effort struggling with unfamiliar terminology and seeking to understand the concerns that motivated our intellectual forbearers. Philosophy can thus be turned into a tour of the past rather than an active inquiry of present importance.

I have known many highly educated persons who studied great works of philosophy, admired the subject, and are pleased when others pursue it. Yet they are unfamiliar with either the concerns or methods of contemporary philosophy. An introductory course is not entirely satisfying if it leaves these matters as unexplored territory.

2

A second approach to introductory philosophy is to combine reading great works of the past with studying several contemporary texts. In this way, students are made aware of the importance of the history of philosophy but also realize that philosophical inquiry is ongoing. Perhaps the syllabus might include Plato's *Euthyphro, Apology, and Crito*, Parts 1 and 2 of Hobbes's *Leviathan*, and Hume's *An Enquiry Concerning Human Understanding*, along with some contemporary books or articles that are among the instructor's favorites.

A potential danger in this approach, however, is that, in jumping from one classic to another, a student hurdles centuries and may lose historical perspective. On the reading list, Hobbes may follow Plato, but in history two millennia intervened, and students unacquainted with any of what occurred in philosophical thought during that period are apt to have a distorted view of how the works of these authors relate. In addition, reading a small number of contemporary authors does not go far in offsetting the view that philosophy is primarily the history of philosophy.

An unusual variation of this approach is to read a single historical text, then analyze it using contemporary methods. Such a plan was presented many years ago by Fred Feldman, when, at a session of the Eastern Division Meeting of the American Philosophical Association, he defended his practice of requiring beginning students to read and critique only one book: Descartes' *Meditations*. The commentator on Feldman's talk was Alasdair MacIntyre, who unintentionally revealed the problem with Feldman's approach by first praising the strategy of focusing on a single work but expressing dismay that Feldman had selected the wrong one. He had chosen Descartes' *Meditations* rather than MacIntyre's choice: Plato's *Republic*.

The problem is that, had MacIntyre been a student in Feldman's course, MacIntyre would have been unhappy spending fifteen weeks discussing a single book that he didn't find especially illuminating, while Feldman would have had the same reaction had he been a student in MacIntyre's course. Too much of a good thing can become boring, and offering introductory students an entire course on one book might even become excruciating. Just as various professors have different interests, so do students. The opportunity for all of them to respond positively to philosophy is increased by providing a variety of perspectives on the subject. A graduate seminar might appropriately focus on a single text, but an introductory course is intended to arouse the interest of as many as possible, and a narrow set of readings is unlikely to achieve that goal.

3

A third format uses a single-authored textbook written with a student audience in mind. The advantage of this approach is that reading a contemporary synopsis of philosophical problems is far easier to understand than trying to grasp original works.

The problem, though, is that, unlike calculus or accounting, philosophy does not offer a body of accepted truths, and one author can hardly do justice to all competing viewpoints. Granted, philosophy can be difficult to understand, and a textbook may ease the strain. On the other hand, philosophical disagreement is best grasped by confronting various authors who have different styles and opinions. Furthermore, a homogenized textbook designed to avoid taking controversial stands is apt to lead readers to wonder why the author appears indecisive.

A key feature of the study of philosophy is that good reasons can be given for opposing positions. Students need to recognize this feature of the subject. When they ask "Who's right?" they should be led to understand that just as each member of a trial jury needs to make a decision and defend a view after considering all relevant evidence, so each philosophical inquirer needs to make a decision and defend a view after considering all relevant arguments.

As stated previously, teachers should offer reliable accounts of positions with which they disagree, but, as Mill observes, we should hear opposing views "from persons who actually believe them, who defend them in earnest, and do their very utmost for them."[1] Because bringing proponents of clashing opinions to the classroom is usually not possible, teachers can at least provide readings in which opposing standpoints are presented as plausibly as possible. Achieving this goal when all views are expressed in one voice is a major challenge.

4

The most popular approach to teaching introductory philosophy is to use an anthology in which readings are grouped by topic and drawn from historical and contemporary sources. Students thereby become acquainted with major problems of philosophy, read important historical and contemporary writing on each subject, and are encouraged to think through issues for themselves. Historical philosophers are given a word but not the last word; contemporary philosophers are seen as innovators but not creators *ex nihilo*.

This approach, however, also has pitfalls. As students shift quickly from Aristotle to Locke to Nozick, they are tempted to treat these authors as contemporaries. Students can also lose hold of the threads that are supposed to connect the selections. Furthermore, excerpts taken out of context can be difficult to understand. Importantly, the approach may do a disservice to major historical figures, because reading a few pages from a philosophical classic is somewhat akin to listening to a few pages from a great symphony—the overall effect is typically disappointing.

Despite these problems, books of readings remain a popular choice for teaching introductory philosophy, because they afford instructors the opportunity to cover many topics and authors, thus displaying the range of philosophical inquiry. Doctoral students, however, are often unfamiliar with the available anthologies and need to be reminded, as I stressed earlier, that these books vary enormously in difficulty. (A graduate department would perform a valuable service by offering sample copies of the most widely used introductory textbooks.)

Over the years, I joined with various colleagues to edit four such collections, but the volume most widely used today is my own Exploring Philosophy: An Introductory Anthology, published by Oxford University Press and currently in its sixth edition. In what follows I shall use that book as background to discuss some topics usually covered in introductory courses.

NOTE

1. Mill, p. 64.

Nine

As most students taking their first philosophy course have no idea, or worse a mistaken idea, of the nature of the subject, the first readings provide an orientation. I like the essay by Monroe and Elizabeth Lane Beardsley[1] because it is remarkably clear and will leave no one behind, but others instructors may prefer starting with Bertrand Russell's inspirational chapter from *The Problems of Philosophy*[2] or Plato's *Defense of Socrates*, which has the advantage of historical and philosophical importance but requires background information that some may not wish to take the time to provide.

But then comes an important decision: which area of philosophy to approach first? One choice is epistemology, although I myself find difficulty motivating students to consider whether the table we sense is the real table. Other instructors may prefer a metaphysical issue, such as the nature of the human mind, but I fear that the complexities of that subject, even in the capable hands of such as Paul M. Churchland,[3] may prove overwhelming.

My preference, instead, is to begin with the elements of reasoning. Every philosophical issue involves argument, and I want to be sure all students are familiar with the concepts of premise, conclusion, validity, and soundness, so that these terms can be used throughout the course.

The key idea, which requires emphasis because it is coun-terintuitive, is that a valid argument can have false premises and a true conclusion. To try to ensure students grasp this point, after explaining it as clearly as I can, I move quickly around the room challenging students:

1. Give me an invalid argument with two true premises and a true conclusion.
2. Give me a valid argument with two false premises and a false conclusion.
3. Give me a valid argument with two false premises and a true conclusion.
4. Give me a valid argument with one false premise and a true conclusion.
5. Give me a valid argument with one true premise, one false premise, and a false conclusion.
6. Give me a valid argument with one true premise, one false premise, and a true conclusion.
7. Give me a valid argument with a true premise and a false conclusion. (You find doing so impossible. Why?)

Soon most students understand the nature of a valid argument and realize the possibility of its having false premises and a true conclusion. The exercise is not unduly taxing, can be enjoyable or even a source of humor, and is accessible to everyone.

Next, I turn to a fallacy that many logic books bypass, but which is committed more frequently than most they discuss. I refer to the confusion of necessary and sufficient condi-tions. How often, for instance, do you hear someone remark that the government can reduce the money allocated for a particular purpose, perhaps national defense or the war on poverty, because even with additional funds success may not be achieved. In other words, more money isn't necessary, because it isn't sufficient.

When I sought a brief article on the subject to include in the anthology, I found none, so I wrote my own that reflects the presentation I would make in class. Of course, I wouldn't deal with the issue by saying to the students, "You all can see that if A is a necessary condition for B, A may not be a sufficient condition for B, so let's move on to more interesting material." I wouldn't classify that approach as *bad* teaching; it isn't even teaching. Telling something to someone who lacks the background to understand what you are saying is just talking, not teaching. Teaching requires communicating, and to communicate is "to make common," that is, "to share," and I haven't shared information with you if you haven't grasped it.

As to how to motivate the discussion of necessary and sufficient conditions, I do so by remarking how often even sophisticated people commit this fallacy. Then I carefully define "necessary condition" and "sufficient condition," providing clear examples of each:

> One state of affairs, A, is a necessary condition for another state of affairs, B, if B cannot occur without A occurring. For instance, in the United States a person must be at least eighteen years old before being entitled to vote. In other words, being eighteen is a necessary condition for being entitled to vote.
>
> One state of affairs, A, is a sufficient condition for another state of affairs, B, if the occurrence of A ensures the occurrence of B. For instance, in an American presidential election for a candidate to receive 300 electoral votes ensures that candidate's election. In other words, receiving 300 electoral votes is a sufficient condition for winning the election.

The next step is to emphasize the difference between necessary and sufficient conditions and provide further examples:

> Note that even if A is a necessary condition for B, A need not be a sufficient condition for B. For instance, even if you need to be eighteen to vote, you also need to be a citizen of the United States. Thus being eighteen is necessary but not sufficient for voting.
>
> Similarly, even if A is a sufficient condition for B, A need not be a necessary condition for B. For instance, if a presidential candidate receives 300 electoral votes, then that candidate is elected, but receiving 300 electoral votes, while sufficient for election, is not necessary, because a candidate who receives 299 votes is also elected.

Now comes an example of how necessary and sufficient conditions may be muddled:

> Confusing necessary and sufficient conditions is a common mistake in reasoning. If one individual argues that extensive prior experience in Washington, DC, is required for a person to be a worthy presidential candidate, that claim is not refuted by pointing out that many candidates with such experience have not been worthy. To refute the claim that experience is necessary for worthiness requires demonstrating not that many with experience have been unworthy but that a person without experience *has* been worthy. After all, the original claim was that experience is necessary, not sufficient.

A further insight is that if you provide necessary and sufficient conditions for a term, then it has been defined:

> Suppose A is both necessary and sufficient for B. For example, being a rectangle with all four sides equal is necessary and sufficient for being a square. In other words, a geomet-

ric figure cannot be a square unless it is a rectangle with
four sides equal, and if a rectangle has all four sides equal,
then it is a square. Thus a satisfactory definition of "square"
is "rectangle with all four sides equal."

The final step in teaching necessary and sufficient conditions is the hardest to grasp, yet essential to understanding the relationship of the two concepts. Before presenting it, I alert students to the challenge it presents:

Here is an additional twist. What is the difference between
asserting that A is a necessary condition for B and that B is
a sufficient condition for A? Nothing. These are two ways of
saying that the occurrence of B ensures the occurrence of
A. Furthermore, what is the difference between asserting
that A is a sufficient condition for B and that B is a necessary
condition for A? Again, nothing. These are two ways of saying
that the occurrence of A ensures the occurrence of B.

For emphasis, I then remind students of the most common error, so they will be less prone to commit it:

The critical mistake is thinking that if A is necessary for B,
then A is sufficient for B. Or that if A is sufficient for B, then
A is necessary for B. These are fallacies, errors in reasoning.

And now to offer one additional example and help students grasp the overall sense of the discussion:

Hence the next time you hear someone say, for example,
that you can be well educated without knowing any logic,
because some people who know logic are not well educated,
you can point out that the speaker has confused necessary
and sufficient conditions. Just because some people who
know logic are not well educated does not prove that you
can be well educated without knowing logic. That conclusion

would only follow if some people who don't know logic are
nevertheless well educated.

 If you're on the lookout for this fallacy, you'll find it
committed far more often than you might suppose.

When the presentation is completed, you can test your students and your own pedagogical skill by asking the class these
questions:

1. If A is a necessary condition for B, is B always a necessary
   condition for A?
2. If A is a necessary condition for B, is B always a sufficient
   condition for A?
3. Is the claim that the study of philosophy is necessary for
   happiness undermined by presenting cases of unhappy
   people who have studied philosophy?
4. Present your own example of the fallacy of confusing necessary and sufficient conditions.

If most students can answer these questions, your teaching
has succeeded. If they can't, then you have failed.

I am not suggesting, of course, that this presentation is
the best or only way of explaining this material. Others may
have a more engaging or effective approach, and I would welcome learning about it.

If, on the other hand, you find such pedagogical matters
of little interest, do not wish to be bothered with offering
elementary explanations, or do not care whether as many students as possible have mastered this sort of basic material,
then regardless of your philosophical ability, you are likely to
be ineffective in the classroom.

And not only for beginning courses. A former colleague of
mine at New York University, Kai Nielsen, was highly regarded

as an undergraduate and graduate teacher, and when asked the key to his success at any level, he replied, "Every course I teach is an introductory course." He meant that no matter how advanced the class was supposed to be, he never proceeded without explaining every step in his reasoning, so no student would become lost. Other celebrated teachers who taught similarly were Roderick Chisholm at Brown University and Rogers Albritton at Harvard University. I heard both lecture, and their clarity was memorable. They weren't in the classroom to flaunt their erudition or display their brilliance; they were there to teach.

NOTES

1. Monroe C. Beardsley and Elizabeth Lane Beardsley, "What Is Philosophy?" in Steven M. Cahn, ed., *Exploring Philosophy: An Introductory Anthology*, Sixth Edition (New York: Oxford University Press, 2018), pp. 3–12.
2. Bertrand Russell, "The Value of Philosophy," in Cahn, pp. 13–15.
3. Paul M. Churchland, "The Mind-Body Problem," in Cahn, pp. 156–168.

Ten

Whichever metaphysical or epistemological issues you choose to discuss will be difficult for beginners. I myself have had most success with the problem of free will and determinism. Its advantages for pedagogical purposes are that it can be briefly presented in the form of an argument with two premises and a conclusion, its most obvious solutions are each plausible but together incompatible, and its connection to issues about moral and legal responsibility can easily be made apparent. The essence of the presentation I offer to students is found in my article "Freedom or Determinism?"[1]

I should first explain, however, that I don't mix my discussion of determinism with the issue of fatalism. Although my earliest full-length work was devoted to that subject,[2] my experience has been that students are bewildered by such matters as Aristotle's doctrine of future contingencies, William of Ockham's views on God's omniscience, and Richard Taylor's controversial proof for the fatalistic conclusion that has engendered so many arguments and counterarguments (including David Foster Wallace's recently published senior thesis at Amherst College).[3] Furthermore, although a fatalist is committed to the conclusion that we have no more control over future events than we have now over past ones, the fatalist does not appeal to an analysis of causation. A determinist, on the other hand, is committed to the principle that every event has a cause, but does not necessarily deny free will. In the face of such potential for confusion, I focus on determinism and leave fatalism for another setting.

To motivate the issue of freedom and determinism, I use the famous 1924 Leopold and Loeb case. I thereby tie the issue to a practical context and illustrate how philosophical issues can arise outside a classroom.

Most students will respond, whether positively or negatively, to Clarence Darrow's appeal on behalf of his precocious teenage clients, who confessed to the murder of Loeb's fourteen-year-old cousin:

> To believe that any boy is responsible for himself or his early training is an absurdity that no lawyer or judge should be guilty of today. . . .
>
> I do not know what remote ancestors have sent down the seed that corrupted him, and I do not know through how many ancestors it may have passed until it reached Dickie Loeb. . . .
>
> I know that if this boy had been understood and properly trained—properly for him—and the training that he got might have been the very best for someone; but if it had been the proper training for him he would not be in this courtroom today with the noose above his head. If there is anywhere responsibility, it is back of him; somewhere in the infinite number of his ancestors, or in his surroundings, or both. And I submit, Your Honor, that under every principle of natural justice, under every principle of conscience, of right, and of law, he should not be made responsible for the acts of someone else.[4]

As happened in the more than one hundred cases in which Darrow defended someone charged with murder, his clients were saved from the death penalty. (On a historical note, immediately after the Leopold and Loeb case, Darrow went to a Dayton, Tennessee, courtroom to be the defense attorney in the trial of John T. Scopes, charged with the crime of teaching evolution.)

The key to Darrow's defense is that, if the argument he utilized is sound, then not only were Leopold and Loeb not to blame for what they had done, but no persons are ever to blame for any of their actions. That observation leads to formulating the basis of Darrow's argument as follows:

Premise 1: No action is free if it must occur.
Premise 2: In the case of every event that occurs, antecedent conditions, known or unknown, ensure the event's occurrence.
Conclusion: Therefore, no action is free.

Here the previous work on validity and soundness comes into play, and the questions can be asked: Is the argument valid? Is it sound? As students will recognize, the argument is valid, because the conclusion follows from the premises, but are the premises true?

If you believe so, then you are, to use the terminology of William James, a "hard determinist."[5] In other words, you accept determinism, believe determinism incompatible with free will, and conclude that human beings never act freely. If, on the other hand, you accept determinism but believe it compatible with free will, then you are a "soft determinist." But what if you believe in free will but don't think that it is compatible with determinism? Then you are a "libertarian."

The upshot is that each of the three agrees partially and disagrees partially with each of the other two. The hard determinist and soft determinist agree that determinism is true but disagree as to whether it is compatible with freedom.

The hard determinist and libertarian agree that the two doctrines are incompatible but disagree as to which is true. The soft determinist and libertarian agree that people have free will but disagree as to whether freedom is compatible with determinism.

One of the three would appear to be correct and the other two wrong. But whose position is most persuasive? Each has a burden to bear.

Hard determinism has to overcome the plausible claim that, for instance, while attending a lecture I have it within my power to raise my hand to ask a question and also have it within my power not to do so. The decision is up to me, but in that case I am free with regard to raising my hand, and hard determinism is refuted.

Soft determinism has to overcome the plausible claim that if my actions are the result of a causal claim extending back before my birth, then I am not now free with regard to any action. Thus determinism and free will are incompatible.

The libertarian has to overcome the plausible claim that every event is caused, whether a loud noise, a change in the weather, or a human action. If the events hadn't been caused, they wouldn't have occurred. Thus because determinism and free will are incompatible and determinism is true, free will is false.

As the class proceeds, we consider each position in turn, discussing whether it can meet the burden it is forced to carry. Can the hard determinist explain the widespread sense that we sometimes act freely? (The reading by Thomas Nagel[6] considers this challenge.) Can the soft determinist demonstrate how determinism and free will can both be true? (The readings from Hume[7] and W. T. Stace[8] are intended to bolster that position.) Can the libertarian explain how human behavior can be understood if it is not caused? Here I appeal to a possible distinction between reasons and causes, suggesting that while causes can explain why a machine malfunctions, only reasons can explain why a human being stops work as a protest.

Thus we end this unit, having tried to make the best possible case for each of the three alternatives and leaving the matter for each student to reach a judgment. The lesson to be drawn is that philosophical questions are perplexing, but to understand the difficulties is a significant step toward strengthening one's ability to think critically about fundamental issues. What if some believe that their solution easily resolves all perplexities? In that case, I would suggest that they haven't fully understood the problem.

NOTES

1. Steven M. Cahn, "Freedom or Determinism," in Cahn, pp. 207–217.
2. Steven M. Cahn, *Fate, Logic, and Time* (New Haven, CT: Yale University Press, 1967), reprinted by Wipf and Stock Publishers, Eugene, OR, 2004.
3. *Fate, Time, and Language: An Essay on Free Will by David Foster Wallace*, eds. Steven M. Cahn and Maureen Eckert (New York: Columbia University Press, 2011).
4. From *The Plea of Clarence Darrow*, August 22nd, 23rd, and 25th, in Defense of Richard Loeb and Nathan Leopold, Jr., On Trial for Murder (Chicago, IL: Ralph Fletcher Seymour, 1924).
5. See William James, "The Dilemma of Determinism," in Cahn, *Exploring Philosophy*, pp. 231–243.
6. Thomas Nagel, "Free Will," in Cahn, *op. cit.*, pp. 199–204.
7. David Hume, "An Enquiry Concerning Human Understanding," in Cahn, *op. cit.*, pp. 223–231.
8. W. T. Stace, "Free Will and Determinism," in Cahn, *op. cit.* pp. 204–206.

Eleven

Recognizing difficulties in one's position is especially challenging in religious matters, and for that reason I prefer turning to that subject only after having explored at least one other issue where personal commitment does not run so deep. In any case, eventually the time comes for discussing aspects of the philosophy of religion. Here motivation is not a problem, because the topic matters so much to so many.

1

The routine approach is to present and assess the three traditional arguments for the existence of God. Then the focus shifts to the problem of evil, after which the unit on God's existence ends.

I want to suggest that this discussion often takes place within a set of misleading assumptions that may be shared by students and faculty members. One of these assumptions is that if God's existence were disproved, then religious commitment would have been shown to be unreasonable. Various religions, however, reject the notion of a supernatural God. These include Jainism, Theravada Buddhism, Mimamsa and Samkhya Hinduism, as well as Reconstructionist Judaism and "Death of God" versions of Christianity.

Here, for example, is how Rabbi Mordecai M. Kaplan, an opponent of supernaturalism, responds to a skeptic who asks why, if the Bible isn't taken literally, Jews should nevertheless observe the Sabbath:

> We observe the Sabbath not so much because of the account
> of its origin in Genesis, as because of the role it has come
> to play in the spiritual life of our People and of mankind. . . .
> The Sabbath day sanctifies our life by what it contributes
> to making us truly human and helping us transcend those
> instincts and passions that are part of our heritage from the
> sub-human.[1]

And here from one of the major figures in the Christian "Death of God" movement, the Anglican Bishop of Woolwich, John A. T. Robinson, who denies the existence of a God "up there," or "out there," is an account of the Holy Communion:

> [T]oo often . . . it ceases to be the holy meal, and becomes
> a religious service in which we turn our backs on the com-
> mon and the community and in individualistic devotion go
> to "make our communion with God out there." This is the
> essence of the religious perversion, when worship becomes
> a realm into which to withdraw from the world to "be with
> God"—even if it is only to receive strength to go back into it.
> In this case the entire realm of the non-religious (in other
> words "life") is relegated to the profane.[2]

Of course, a naturalistic religion can also be developed without deriving it from a supernatural religion. Consider, for example, the outlook of philosopher Charles Frankel, another opponent of supernaturalism, who nevertheless believes that religion, shorn of irrationality, can make a distinctive contribution to human life by providing deliverance from vanity, triumph over meanness, and endurance in the face of tragedy. As he writes, "it seems to me not impossible that a religion could draw the genuine and passionate adherence of its members while it claimed nothing more than to be poetry in which [people] might participate and from which they might draw strength and light."[3]

Such naturalistic options are philosophically respectable. Whether to choose any of them is for each person to decide.

Teachers and students should also recognize that theism does not imply religious commitment. After all, even if someone believes that one or more of the proofs for God's existence is sound, the question remains whether to join a religion and, if so, which one. The proofs contain not a clue as to which religion, if any, is favored by God. Indeed, God may oppose all religious activity. Perhaps God does not wish to be prayed to, worshipped, or adored, and might even reward those who shun such activities.

Yet another misleading assumption is implicit in the definitions that are usually offered: a theist believes in God, an atheist disbelieves in God, and an agnostic neither believes nor disbelieves in God. Notice that the only hypothesis being considered is the existence of God as traditionally conceived; no other supernatural alternatives are taken seriously. But why not?

Suppose, for example, that the world is the scene of a struggle between God and the Demon. Both are powerful, but neither is omnipotent. When events go well, God's benevolence is ascendant; when events go badly, the Demon's malevolence is ascendant. Is this doctrine, historically associated width Zoroastrianism and Manichaeism, unnecessarily complex and therefore to be rejected? No, for even though the dualistic hypothesis is in a way more complex than monotheism, involving two supernatural beings rather than one, in another sense the dualistic hypothesis is simpler, because it leaves no aspect of the world beyond human understanding."

After all, theism faces the problem of evil, while the dualistic hypothesis has no difficulty accounting for both good and evil.

In short, I would suggest that both faculty members and students should remember the following four essential points: (1) belief in the existence of God is not a necessary condition for religious commitment; (2) belief in the existence of God is not a sufficient condition for religious commitment; (3) the existence of God is not the only supernatural hypothesis worth serious discussion; and (4) a successful defense of traditional theism requires not only that it be more plausible than atheism or agnosticism but that it be more plausible than all other supernatural alternatives.

I am not suggesting, of course, that the proofs for the existence of God or the problem of evil not be taught. I am urging, however, that all participants be alerted to the limited implications of that discussion.

2

The one historical book in philosophy of religion that is found in abbreviated form in almost every introductory anthology is Hume's *Dialogues Concerning Natural Religion*. Yet because the main points of this masterpiece can be elusive, let me offer a few suggestions on guiding students in approaching the work.

"Natural religion" was the term used by eighteenth-century writers to refer to theological tenets provable by reason without appeal to revelation. The three participants in the *Dialogues* are distinguished by their views concerning the scope and limits of reason. Cleanthes claims he can present arguments that demonstrate the truth of traditional Christian theology. Demea is committed to that theology but does not believe empirical evidence can provide any defense for his faith. Philo doubts that reason yields conclusive results in any field of inquiry and is especially critical of theological dogmatism.

Readers might anticipate that because Demea and Cleanthes are both theists, their positions will be mutually supportive. Matters, however, are not so simple, and students need to be alerted to the sophisticated interplay among the characters.

Remember that the *Dialogues* is a work of fiction, an account offered by one literary character, Pamphilus, to another, Hermippus, of a discussion Pamphilus says he heard one summer day at the house of his teacher Cleanthes. As in any sophisticated drama, we are not simply told the point; we are shown it.

Some lessons, however, are obvious. The most widely used arguments for the existence of God are subjected to trenchant criticisms. In particular, the claim that the structure of the world provides clear evidence of God's handiwork, the so-called "teleological argument," is shown to lack cogency.

Hume, however, not only undermines arguments for the existence of God but also develops in detail what is perhaps the strongest argument against the existence of God, namely, the problem of evil. How can evil exist in a world created by an all-good, all-powerful God? No glib dismissal of this perplexing problem can survive a careful reading of Hume's work.

But more is going on in the *Dialogues* than an examination of arguments for and against the existence of God. Indeed, the three central characters agree that "the question can never be concerning the *being* but only the *nature* of the Deity" (2, 3).[4] Yet how can we make sense of the view that something exists if all its attributes are unknown? Thus the initial agreement among Cleanthes, Demea, and Philo that God exists is of no significance unless they come to some understanding of God's nature.

They cannot do so, however, for when the traditional arguments for the existence of God have been shown to afford no understanding of the Divine, and the problem of evil forces the believer to seek refuge in God's incomprehensibility, theism loses its meaning. I would propose this insight as the underlying theme of the *Dialogues*.

Hume's genius is demonstrated in the development of this motif, for by subtle and realistic interplay among his three main characters, he brings to light the surprising affinity between the skeptic and the person of faith, as well as the lack of affinity between the person of faith and the philosophical theist.

For example, at the opening of Part 2, Demea states that God's nature is "altogether incomprehensible and unknown to us" (2, 1). Philo agrees and speaks of "the adorably mysterious and incomprehensible nature of the Supreme Being" (2, 4). Cleanthes, however, recognizes that these views render theism vacuous, and so he immediately launches into a statement of the teleological argument, thereby attempting to provide some understanding of the ways of God. Cleanthes's conclusion is that "the Author of nature is somewhat similar to the mind of man" (3, 5).

But when Philo criticizes Cleanthes's analogy, Demea, who is suspicious of any attempt to describe the Supreme Being, sides with Philo, arguing that "the infirmities of our nature do not permit us to reach any ideas which in the least correspond to the ineffable sublimity of the Divine attributes" (3, 13). Cleanthes warns Demea that if he persists in maintaining that God is completely unknowable, he will rob theism of any sense, but Demea does not grasp this point, and, with Philo's encouragement, continues to defend his self-defeating position.

In part 9, after Philo has completed his ferocious attack on Cleanthes's version of the teleological argument, Demea suggests that they rely on the cosmological or first cause argument. By placing this attempted proof in the mouth of Demea, Hume emphasizes that even the most ardent partisans of faith have recourse to reason when defending their position. Furthermore, Hume is suggesting that those who affirm the incomprehensibility of God do not quite mean what they say, because they are prepared to try to offer some description of the Divine, even if it be so abstract a one as "necessarily existent Being . . . which determined *something* to exist rather than *nothing*" (9, 3).

Demea's argument is initially undermined not by Philo but by Cleanthes, who argues that the phrase "necessary existence" has no meaning and, furthermore, that no sense can be given to the notion of a first cause that is supposed to stand apart from the entire causal chain. Cleanthes's willingness to deny significance to Demea's concept of God serves as a reminder that anyone who enters the arena of reason is subject to attack by all those committed to rationality, be they theists or atheists.

In Part 10, where the subject of discussion turns to the evils in the world, Cleanthes again finds himself opposing Philo and Demea, both of whom defend the view that "the whole earth . . . is cursed and polluted" (10, 8). Cleanthes realizes that Philo can utilize the ills of the world to discredit the existence of a God who is all-good and all-powerful, but Demea fails to appreciate this difficulty, for he is confident that present evils will be rectified at some other time and place.

Cleanthes, however, is appalled by this line of reasoning, because it amounts to nothing more than trying to explain away the damaging evidence of evil by appeal to an arbitrary supposition about an unknown afterlife. Cleanthes understands, as Demea does not, that taking a leap of faith in the face of strong evidence to the contrary raises serious doubts about the very meaningfulness of one's faith.

If God's love for humanity is compatible with our being forced to endure the most terrible miseries, then what exactly is the significance of the claim that God loves us? How would things be different if God didn't love us?

Cleanthes attempts to defend the goodness of the world, hoping thereby to bolster the theistic position he and Demea share. But Philo, using evidence in part originally supplied by Demea, easily overwhelms Cleanthes, and Demea finally realizes that his apparent ally through much of the discussion has all along been his most dangerous enemy.

In Part 12, after Demea has become upset and left the company, Philo tries to soothe the displeasure exhibited by his host, Cleanthes. Many commentators have found this section puzzling, because Philo proceeds to agree with Cleanthes that the universe exhibits purpose. The reader should have been aware by this point, however, that Philo's apparently theistic utterances are not all they seem to be, and Philo soon reveals the insignificance of his admission.

In the end he adopts the view that the whole of natural religion is reducible to one proposition: "*That the cause or causes of order in the universe probably bear some remote analogy to human intelligence*" (12, 33). Yet because the import of this statement is negated by such qualifications as "cause or causes," "probably," and "remote analogy," the claim is at bottom neither theistic nor atheistic but simply devoid of clear sense. We are left only with Philo's observation that the proposition "affords no inference that affects human life" (12, 33). This conclusion, if accepted, sounds the death knell for traditional theology.

In the final sentence of the book, we are told that "Philo's principles are more probable than Demea's, but that those of Cleanthes approach still nearer to the truth" (12, 34). Those who assume this summation to be Hume's find it perplexing, because so many of Cleanthes's arguments have been undermined throughout the work. The statement, however, is not Hume's but that of the narrator Pamphilus, who, as a student of Cleanthes, understandably finds Cleanthes's position the most persuasive of the three.

Why should Hume have ended the *Dialogues* with a misleading assessment of the discussion? The answer is that eighteenth-century English society did not take kindly to attacks on traditional theological tenets. Because Hume had no desire to precipitate a scandal, he adopted the literary device of a narrator who at both the beginning and the end could assure suspicious readers that, regardless of what might appear to have happened in the *Dialogues*, theism is triumphant.

Indeed, Hume's friends were so fearful of the public's disapproval that, despite his precautions, they dissuaded him from publishing the manuscript. Fortunately, he took great pains to assure the work would not be lost, and it appeared in print three years after his death, although without any publisher's name attached.

Never before or since has traditional Christian theology faced more dangerous philosophical attacks. Whether it can be plausibly defended in the face of such profound challenges is a matter that students need to decide for themselves.

NOTES

1. Mordecai M. Kaplan, *Judaism Without Supernaturalism* (New York: Reconstructionist Press, 1958), pp. 115–116.
2. John A. T. Robinson, *Honest to God* (Philadelphia, PA: Westminster, 1963), pp. 86–87.
3. Charles Frankel, *The Love of Anxiety, and Other Essays* (New York: Harper & Row, 1965), p. 1962.
4. David Hume, *Dialogues Concerning Natural Religion and Other Writings*, ed. Dorothy Coleman (New York: Cambridge University Press, 2007). All references are to part-number and paragraph-number.

Twelve

When an introductory course arrives at the study of ethics, students are apt to embrace, without recognizing any of the associated difficulties, simplistic forms of subjectivism, relativism, egoism, or divine command theory. Thus explaining these views and pointing out the problems they raise is an effective starting-point. But the question then arises: If no easy answer will do, how can we reason about morality?

Some students will be prepared to believe that, just as we are subject to scientific laws, such as that water freezes at zero degrees centigrade and boils at one hundred degrees centigrade, so murder is wrong and honesty is right. Moreover, just as laws of nature apply at any time and in any place, so do moral laws. The only difference is that laws of nature are tested by scientific method, while moral laws are tested by conscience.

This theory, however, runs into troubles that other students will quickly point out. First, moral laws can be broken, whereas scientific laws cannot. A person can steal a book, thereby breaking a moral law, but cannot succeed in tossing a book into the air and prevent its being subject to the law of gravity. Second, the dictates of one person's conscience may conflict with those of another. How can we decide between them? We can appeal to the dictates of our own conscience, but ours may be biased. Or we can appeal to the dictates of the conscience of the majority, but theirs may also be mistaken. After all, moral principles are not decided by vote.

Perhaps, then, moral judgments aren't true or false but merely express preferences, thus leading back to subjectivism or relativism. Yet students need to be reminded that, faced with social injustice, they attempt to demonstrate its unfairness. Therefore reasoning does appear to have a role in arriving at conclusions about right and wrong.

Given this metaethical impasse, how to proceed? One approach that is often overlooked is to try to understand the nature of moral judgments by considering some value claims unrelated to ethics. For instance, we speak of "a good restaurant," or "the bad television reception." How are these statements justified?

Here is the opportunity to work through a specific example. I've had success using sports, but some may find that other cases work as well or better. My favorite hypothetical is to suppose you are a member of a softball league. Your friend Beth tells you that Susan is an excellent ballplayer, so you ask her to join your team, but she turns out to be woefully inadequate. She drops balls thrown to her, lets ground balls go through her legs, and strikes out almost every time she comes to bat. You tell Beth that her recommendation of Susan was a mistake. Either Beth does not know how to judge a good ballplayer, or someone has misled her about Susan's abilities, because obviously Susan is not a good ballplayer.

Notice that when you say that Susan is not a good ballplayer, you are neither appealing to the dictates of conscience nor expressing an arbitrary preference. Rather, you are basing your judgment on the facts—facts about softball, not facts about goodness. The reason Susan is not a good ballplayer is that she hits poorly and fields inadequately. To defend your view, all you need do is point to Susan's batting and fielding averages. While disagreement may persist if Susan hits .250 and commits a few errors, without doubt a ballplayer who hits .150 and commits errors in every game is not a good ballplayer, whereas one who hits .350 and rarely commits an error is a good ballplayer. The distinction is clear, despite the possibility of borderline cases, just as the distinction between bald and hirsute is clear despite disputable instances.

Note that if Susan hits and fields well, someone would be confused to wonder if Susan might still lack one attribute essential to a good ballplayer, namely goodness, because if Susan hits and fields well, then she is a good ballplayer. Goodness is not another attribute besides hitting and fielding well but a shorthand way of referring to those skills.

Suppose when you tell Beth that Susan is not a good ballplayer, Beth agrees that Susan doesn't hit or field well, but Beth argues that a good ballplayer is one who is obliging to fans. She claims that because Susan has this attribute, she is a good ballplayer.

While Beth's reply would be exasperating, you could respond by emphasizing that the criteria for a good ballplayer are not arbitrary. You play softball to win; hence good players are those who help in winning. Susan does not do so and therefore is not a good ballplayer.

If Beth thinks players who are obliging to fans help the team win, her view can be disproven by an appeal to the record books. But if Beth believes softball is played not to win but to gain popularity, then players who are obliging to fans may be more effective in achieving that aim. In that case, however, Beth's recommendations of ballplayers would be of no value to the overwhelming number of participants whose aim in playing the game is to score more runs than the opposition.

We have extended this example far enough to clarify the nature of non-moral value judgments. First, although the term "good" is a term of commendation, the criteria for its use vary depending on the context and our purposes. Good apples, good computers, and good ballplayers are good for different reasons. Second, if two people disagree about a value judgment but agree on the criteria for goodness, then the disagreement is in principle resolvable by the use of empirical testing procedures. Third, if the two individuals disagree about a value judgment and also disagree on the criteria for goodness, then the two need to consider why they have chosen their differing criteria. If the people can find a basis for agreement on further ends that are supposed to justify the criteria, then the disagreement is again in principle resolvable by the use of empirical testing procedures. If, however, the ends are fundamentally incompatible, then the disagreement will not yield to rational resolution.

An obvious question that students will raise is: What are the chances that in a moral disagreement the disputants will agree on ends? At first glance, searching for consensus might appear hopeless, but it may be found by recognizing that we depend on others to achieve our most valued goals. As Jonathan Harrison observes:

> We cannot conceive of a being like ourselves, who desires his own happiness, and the happiness of his family and friends (if not the happiness of the whole of mankind), who needs the company of his fellows, who is easily injured by their hostile acts, and who cannot continue to exist unless they co-operate with him—we cannot conceive of a being such as this approving of promise-breaking, dishonesty, and deliberate callousness to the interests of others.[1]

In short, our humanity requires that we rely on others, and therefore we approve of actions that facilitate cooperation.

Any individual who rejects this way of thinking and instead favors persecution and cruelty for their own sake is not to be argued with but to be guarded against. Interestingly, no political leader has ever come to power by promising to increase hatred, violence, and oppression. To gain public support, even the worst of dictators mouths the usual moral sentiments.

Thus if a moral skeptic should inquire why we should be concerned about the welfare of others, we can do no better than offer the response James Rachels provides: "The reason one ought not to do actions that would hurt other people is: other people would be hurt. The reason one ought to do actions that would benefit other people is: other people would be benefitted." If such considerations count for nothing, then the discussion is over. But what if someone insistently maintains a position in favor of immorality? Then, quoting Rachels again:

> he is saying something quite extraordinary. He is saying that he has no affection for friends or family, that he never feels pity or compassion, that he is the sort of person who can look on scenes of human misery with complete indifference, so long as he is not the one suffering. . . . Indeed, a man without any sympathy would scarcely be recognizable as a man.[2]

The result is that a commitment to immorality is unlikely to be defended by anyone except an obstinate student in a philosophy seminar, who nevertheless expects to receive kind consideration and an equitable grade, never noticing that these reflect a concern for ethical treatment.

Moral philosophy includes normative ethics, metaethics, and moral problems. How much of that material can be covered in an introductory course depends on the judgment of the instructor, but most important is for students to realize that thinking clearly about morality is important, yet demanding. Anyone who believes moral philosophy is easy compared to epistemology or philosophy of language does not fully appreciate the difficulties inherent in developing a satisfactory ethical theory. Indeed, a youngster is far more likely to contribute a major insight into logic or philosophy of mathematics than to provide a deepened understanding of the moral sphere.

NOTES

1. Jonathan Harrison, "Empiricism in Ethics," *Philosophical Quarterly* 2:9 (1952), p. 306.
2. James Rachels, "Egoism and Moral Skepticism," in Cahn, *op. cit.*, pp. 363–364.

Thirteen

By this point in the course, students have realized that philosophy calls into doubt widely agreed-upon beliefs. The importance of doing so was famously stressed by John Stuart Mill, who writes:

> if the received opinion be not only true, but the whole truth; unless it is suffered to be, and actually is, vigorously and earnestly contested, it will, by most of those who receive it, be held in the manner of a prejudice, with little comprehension or feeling of its rational grounds.[1]

In our society, the received opinion in the political arena is the superiority of democracy over all other systems. To keep that view from turning into a mere prejudice, however, it needs to be challenged, and I know of no work that does so more effectively than Plato's *Republic*. While that remarkable book offers a unified account of central issues in metaphysics, epistemology, philosophy of mind, ethics, social philosophy, philosophy of art, and philosophy of education, the work makes as powerful a case as any against democracy, thus providing a gateway into the study of the political realm.

Before introducing Plato, you might ask students to consider the following scenario. You go to a polling place on election day. There, waiting to cast ballots, are the various members of the community—a carpenter, a gardener, a lawyer, a bus driver, a piano tuner, and an artist. Each has one vote, and the will of the majority prevails.

Standing in line, we might imagine, is Archie Bunker, the engaging but ill-informed and bigoted figure in the classic television sitcom *All in the Family*, Were Archie asked about his preferences, he might reply that he has no idea who is running in this election, but it makes no difference to him, because he has voted for the same party his entire life and has no intention of ever switching. As for the bond issue that appears in the upper right-hand corner of the voting machine, he hadn't realized it was there, but now that you've mentioned it, he'll be sure to vote against it, because he votes against all bond issues as a waste of money. (If Archie strikes students as a caricature, you might remind them that politicians always seek to place their names at the top of the ballot, because a sizable number of voters select whichever name is first, apparently believing that higher is better.)

Standing behind Archie is a professor of political science who has devoted her life to a study of the American political system. She may be familiar with the views of every candidate and even have helped formulate the exact wording of the bond issue. Yet, like Archie, she receives only one vote; her erudition entitles her to nothing more.

Does this arrangement make sense? After all, if you visit a physician seeking advice as to whether to undergo an operation, you would be appalled if the doctor explained that the policy in that office was to poll a random sample of passersby and act in accordance with the will of the majority. A community would be similarly dismayed if it hired an engineer to build a bridge, and the engineer announced that deciding how deeply to lay the foundations would be decided by a vote of the townspeople. In short, to deal with medical or engineering problems, we seek expert judgment, not the uninformed opinions of the populace. Why, then, faced with political problems, do we take the issue to all the people rather than to specialists?

Here you can introduce Plato, pointing out that he considered this same question. Believing no answer to be reasonable, he proceeded to construct a system of government based on the view that issues of political policy, being complex, technical matters, ought to be placed in the hands of experts. The Platonic utopia, therefore, was to be ruled by a small group of philosopher-kings, chosen on the basis of their aptitudes and educated for their roles. Most members of society were to be tradespeople: the farmer was expected only to farm, the cobbler only to cobble. They were to play no role in the governance of the state, and their education was to be in the narrowest sense a trade education.

Indeed, from Plato's viewpoint, even to suggest that farmers or cobblers should participate in the affairs of government would have been a grave mistake, for the farmer was fitted only to farm, the cobbler fitted only to cobble. The philosopher-kings were fitted to rule, and they would do so most effectively if not interfered with by those ill-suited to deliberate about decisions affecting the future of their society.

You might emphasize Plato's comparing the workings of a democratic society to the situation aboard a ship on which the sailors are arguing over the control of the helm, while none has ever learned navigation. If someone happens to possess the needed skills, that person's qualifications will be disregarded on the grounds that steering a ship requires no special competence. Plato scornfully observes that "with a magnificent indifference to the sort of life a person has led before he enters politics . . . [a democracy] will promote to honor anyone who merely calls himself the people's friend."[2]

To ensure that those who will serve as philosopher-kings are qualified to take on their responsibilities, Plato requires that prospective office-holders embark on a rigorous intellectual program, topped off by the study of dialectic, that is, explicating key concepts in the light of a vision of the good. No doubt many today would be more inclined to concentrate such advanced education for political leadership less on the intricacies of abstract reasoning and more on issues in political science, economics, sociology, and international relations. The force of Plato's proposal, however, is not found in the specifics of the curriculum he proposes but in the notion that office-holders should be required to receive intellectual preparation for their positions.

Do students accept this idea? Do they favor government by experts? Perhaps, instead, they would agree with the late conservative writer William F. Buckley, Jr., who remarked, "I should sooner live in a society governed by the first two thousand names in the Boston telephone directory than in a society governed by the two thousand faculty members of Harvard University."

These questions are apt to lead students to engage in spirited discussion about the strengths and weaknesses of the democratic system. Skeptics, however, should be reminded that by whatever procedures the rulers of an aristocracy are selected, mistakes are possible, and as the events of history have so often demonstrated, once unrestrained authority is placed in the wrong hands, the results are likely to be calamitous. In a democracy, a foolish decision made on one occasion can be undone on another, but when all control has been transferred to the aristocrats, second chances are no longer possible. Members of a democracy avoid having to make the difficult, dangerous, and unalterable decision of whom to entrust with unrestricted power.

Furthermore, even if the rulers are initially kindhearted, in time they tend to lose touch with the ruled. Even the best-intentioned of sovereigns may find difficulty remaining sensitive to the needs and desires of those under their control.

Although an elite may possess greater expertise in certain technical matters than do other individuals, members of a society possess special insight into their own problems, interests, and goals. As John Dewey points out, "the individuals of the submerged mass may not be very wise. But there is one thing they are wiser about than anybody else can be, and that is where the shoe pinches, the troubles they suffer from."[3] Only the democratic system ensures that this self-knowledge is taken into account in the governmental process.

A democratic society, moreover, is distinguished by the quality of life inherent in its procedures. Competitive elections require the expression of opposing points of view, and the protection of the right of all citizens to speak freely, write freely, and assemble freely, thus producing a vitality than enriches all.

For such reasons, Winston Churchill suggested that democracy is the worst form of government except for all the others that have been tried. Would Plato have been sympathetic to this claim?

Students will be surprised to learn that the answer is "yes," but he expressed that view not in *The Republic* but in what is widely thought to be a later dialogue, namely, *The Statesman*. There, near the end of the work, Plato compares three types of government: monarchy, the rule of one; aristocracy, the rule of a few; and democracy, the rule of all.

Plato maintains that if the monarch is ideal, possessing moral and intellectual insight and treating all persons fairly, then monarchy is the best form of government. If, however, the monarch does not govern wisely, then monarchy can degenerate into tyranny, the worst form of government. Similarly, if a small group of rulers always governs wisely, then aristocracy is the second-best form of government. But if the aristocracy does not govern wisely, then it can degenerate into oligarchy, the second worst form of government.

According to Plato, the advantage of democracy is that it is capable of no great good or any serious evil. Thus in a society like ours that is not perfectly law-abiding and in which all do not always carry out their responsibilities appropriately, the best form of government, according to Plato, is—democracy. Despite its faults, it carries the fewest dangers and thus is the wisest choice.

The case for democracy can thus be supported, and Plato can be credited with a deeper understanding of the realities of politics than his critics often suppose. Furthermore, if as a result of this presentation students want to read more of Plato's *Dialogues*, so much the better.

NOTES

1. Mill, p. 83.
2. *The Republic of Plato*, trans. Francis MacDonald Cornford (New York: Oxford University Press, 1945), Book VIII, p. 558.
3. John Dewey, "Democracy," in Cahn, *op. cit.*, pp. 543–547.

Fourteen

In stressing the importance of teaching, I recognize that I am running counter to prevailing practices. After all, although college and university administrators frequently claim to care deeply about the matter, their policies belie their principles.

For instance, which candidate for a faculty position is usually viewed as more attractive, the promising researcher or the promising teacher? Who usually is given the larger salary increase, the successful researcher or the successful teacher? When a faculty member receives an offer from another institution, is more effort usually made to retain an outstanding researcher or an outstanding teacher? Who usually receives such invitations, the famed researcher or the famed teacher? The answers are obvious.

If presidents, provosts, and deans were as concerned about teaching as they claim, their commitment would be demonstrated by policies quite different from those typically now in place.

First, during a campus interview, a candidate for a faculty position would be expected to give not only a research paper but also a talk on an elementary topic, organized and presented as if for introductory students. Only those candidates whose teaching performance was proficient would be taken seriously for an appointment.

Second, when salary raises were distributed, excellence in teaching would be weighed as heavily as excellence in research. Granted, an institution may give teaching awards to a select few while rewarding research for the many, but virtually unheard of is giving research prizes to a select few while rewarding teaching for the many.

Third, just as research is evaluated by peer review, so teaching would be. Popularity among students is a positive sign for a teacher, just as having a book on the Best-Seller List is a positive sign for a researcher, but neither accomplishment ensures academic quality. We care enough about research to undertake an elaborate review of a professor's scholarship; we should care enough about teaching to undertake an equally rigorous review of a professor's work in the classroom. Such a study should involve input from departmental colleagues who would visit the professor's classes and evaluate syllabi, examinations, and term papers. In sum, the more an institution is concerned about teaching, the more effort will be made to assess it.

Fourth, a corollary of serious evaluation of teaching is the willingness to differentiate among levels of effectiveness. We recognize differences between research that is incompetent, barely competent, mediocre, strong, or superb; the same distinctions apply to teaching. Not every sound researcher is a serious candidate for a Nobel Prize or its equivalent; neither is every sound teacher a serious candidate for a teaching Hall of Fame. Describing all teachers as merely "good" or "not so good" is a sign that teaching is not taken seriously. An individual may be said to be a good teacher, but a key question is: how good?

Fifth, an outstanding researcher may be awarded tenure even with a weak performance in the classroom. An analogous policy should be in effect for an outstanding teacher with a thin record in research. While the ideal candidate excels as researcher and teacher, if an occasional exception is made in order not to lose a researcher of national stature, so an occasional exception should also be made for a teacher of similar accomplishment.

Sixth, an institution sometimes seeks to recruit an outstanding researcher to enable a department to enhance its national reputation. Has any school, however, ever recruited an outstanding teacher to enable a department to strengthen its offerings to students? I don't recall ever seeing an announcement seeking such an individual, but a school committed to teaching would from time to time conduct such searches.

Seventh, if administrators cared about teaching, they would champion a course in methods of teaching for all students who are to be recommended for faculty appointments. As I mentioned earlier, such courses should involve future professors in discussing and practicing all phases of the teaching process, including motivating students, organizing and clarifying materials, guiding classes along productive paths, constructing examinations, and grading papers. Emphasis should also be placed on the crucial importance and multi-faceted nature of a teacher's ethical obligations.

Eighth, letters of evaluation would be expected to provide details not only about a candidate's research but also about the candidate's teaching. At present, such letters usually contain a perfunctory sentence or two, assuring the reader that although the writer has never actually seen the candidate teach, given the candidate's intelligence and winning personality, the writer is sure that the candidate will be effective with students. Such expressions of support would be more persuasive if corroborated by personal accounts of classroom performance.

Ninth, just as faculty members are given release time to pursue their research, so they would be supported to develop new courses, syllabi, and methodologies. They would also be given the opportunity to attend a center for teaching effectiveness, working under the guidance of master teachers to strengthen pedagogical skills.

Tenth and finally, at a school seriously concerned with teaching, classrooms would be open to all qualified persons, including any interested members of the faculty who wish to sit in. Physicians watch other physicians conduct medical procedures, thereby honing their own skills; similarly, teachers can learn by observation. Furthermore, teachers who may be visited by peers are apt to devote greater attention to presentations. Open classrooms thus benefit all.

At schools where these policies were in effect, teaching would not be overshadowed by research. Instead, teaching would be taken seriously. And at such institutions, those who pay tuition bills could depend on receiving the quality of instruction to which they are entitled.

Yet I recognize that schools are unlikely to adopt many of the suggestions I have offered. Hence matters lie in the hands of individual instructors. Their reward for effective teaching will be the satisfaction of fulfilling responsibilities and the appreciation of those who are depending on them to do so.

Assuming you care, however, what can you do to improve your teaching? Let me conclude with one simple suggestion. Arrange with a colleague to visit each other's class. The observer should not participate but afterward should discuss all aspects of the proceedings: how a question was well put, how discussion may have gone off the track, whether the instructor was audible, whether writing on the chalkboard was visible, how a difficult concept might have been presented more clearly, or how the motivation might have been strengthened. After your colleague provides this feedback, you should do the same for your colleague. The experience will almost surely be revelatory for both of you, and the results will be especially appreciated by your students. After all, they deserve the best instruction you can provide.

Steven M. Cahn is Professor Emeritus of Philosophy at the City University of New York Graduate Center, where he served for nearly a decade as Provost and Vice President for Academic Affairs, then as Acting President.

He was born in Springfield, Massachusetts, in 1942, and earned his AB from Columbia College in 1963 and his PhD in philosophy from Columbia University in 1966. After having taught religious studies to grade school students, he embarked on a professorial career that included positions at Dartmouth College (then with all-male undergraduates), Vassar College (then with all-female undergraduates), New York University, and the University of Vermont, where he chaired the Department of Philosophy.

He served as a program officer at the Exxon Education Foundation, as Acting Director for Humanities at the Rockefeller Foundation, and as the first Director of General Programs at the National Endowment for the Humanities. He formerly chaired the American Philosophical Association's Committee on the Teaching of Philosophy, was the Association's Delegate to the American Council of Learned Societies, and was longtime President of The John Dewey Foundation.

He is the author or editor of more than fifty books, including the widely used anthologies *Exploring Ethics*, now in its fourth edition; *Exploring Philosophy*, now in its sixth edition; and *Classics of Western Philosophy*, now in its eighth edition.

A collection of essays written in his honor, edited by two of his former doctoral students, Robert B. Talisse of Vanderbilt University and Maureen Eckert of the University of Massachusetts Dartmouth, is titled *A Teacher's Life: Essays for Steven M. Cahn*.

BOOKS AUTHORED

Fate, Logic, and Time
    Yale University Press, 1967
    Ridgeview Publishing Company, 1982
    Wipf and Stock Publishers, 2004

A New Introduction to Philosophy
    Harper & Row, 1971
    University Press of America, 1986
    Wipf and Stock Publishers, 2004

The Eclipse of Excellence: A Critique of American Higher Education
    (Foreword by Charles Frankel)
    Public Affairs Press, 1973
    Wipf and Stock Publishers, 2004

Education and the Democratic Ideal
    Nelson-Hall Company, 1979
    Wipf and Stock Publishers, 2004

Saints and Scamps: Ethics in Academia
    Rowman & Littlefield, 1986
    Revised Edition, 1994
    25th Anniversary Edition, 2011
    (Foreword by Thomas H. Powell)

Philosophical Explorations: Freedom, God, and Goodness
    Prometheus Books, 1989

Puzzles & Perplexities: Collected Essays
    Rowman & Littlefield, 2002
    Second Edition, Lexington Books, 2007

God, Reason, and Religion
    Thomson/Wadsworth, 2006

From Student to Scholar: A Candid Guide to Becoming a Professor
> (Foreword by Catharine R. Stimpson)
> Columbia University Press, 2008

Polishing Your Prose: How to Turn First Drafts Into Finished Work
> (with Victor L. Cahn)
> (Foreword by Mary Ann Caws)
> Columbia University Press, 2013

Happiness and Goodness: Philosophical Reflections on Living Well
> (with Christine Vitrano)
> (Foreword by Robert B. Talisse)
> Columbia University Press, 2015

Religion Within Reason
> Columbia University Press, 2017

Inside Academia: Professors, Politics, and Policies
> Rutgers University Press, 2018

Teaching Philosophy: A Guide
> Routledge, 2018

BOOKS EDITED

Philosophy of Art and Aesthetics: From Plato to Wittgenstein
> (with Frank A. Tillman)
> Harper & Row, 1969

The Philosophical Foundations of Education
> Harper & Row, 1970

Philosophy of Religion
> Harper & Row, 1970

Classics of Western Philosophy
> Hackett Publishing Company, 1977
> Second Edition, 1985
> Third Edition, 1990
> Fourth Edition, 1995
> Fifth Edition, 1999
> Sixth Edition, 2003
> Seventh Edition, 2007
> Eighth Edition, 2012

New Studies in the Philosophy of John Dewey
> University Press of New England, 1977

Scholars Who Teach: The Art of College Teaching
   Nelson-Hall Company, 1978
   Wipf and Stock Publishers, 2004
Contemporary Philosophy of Religion
   (with David Shatz)
   Oxford University Press, 1982
Reason at Work: Introductory Readings in Philosophy
   (with Patricia Kitcher and George Sher)
   Harcourt Brace Jovanovich, 1984
   Second Edition, 1990
   Third Edition (also with Peter J. Markie), 1995
Morality, Responsibility, and the University: Studies in Academic Ethics
   Temple University Press, 1990
Affirmative Action and the University: A Philosophical Inquiry
   Temple University Press, 1993
Twentieth-Century Ethical Theory
   (with Joram G. Haber)
   Prentice Hall, 1995
The Affirmative Action Debate
   Routledge, 1995
   Second Edition, 2002
Classics of Modern Political Theory: Machiavelli to Mill
   Oxford University Press, 1997
Classic and Contemporary Readings in the Philosophy of Education
   McGraw Hill, 1997
   Second Edition, Oxford University Press, 2012
Ethics: History, Theory, and Contemporary Issues
   (with Peter Markie)
   Oxford University Press, 1998
   Second Edition, 2002
   Third Edition, 2006
   Fourth Edition, 2009
   Fifth Edition, 2012
   Sixth Edition, 2015
Exploring Philosophy: An Introductory Anthology
   Oxford University Press, 2000
   Second Edition, 2005

Third Edition, 2009
Fourth Edition, 2012
Fifth Edition, 2015
Sixth Edition, 2018
Classics of Political and Moral Philosophy
Oxford University Press, 2002
Second Edition, 2012
Questions About God: Today's Philosophers Ponder the Divine
(with David Shatz)
Oxford University Press, 2002
Morality and Public Policy
(with Tziporah Kasachkoff)
Prentice Hall, 2003
Knowledge and Reality
(with Maureen Eckert and Robert Buckley)
Prentice Hall, 2003
Philosophy for the 21st Century: A Comprehensive Reader
Oxford University Press, 2003
Ten Essential Texts in the Philosophy of Religion
Oxford University Press, 2005
Political Philosophy: The Essential Texts
Oxford University Press, 2005
Second Edition, 2011
Third Edition, 2015
Philosophical Horizons: Introductory Readings
(with Maureen Eckert)
Thomson/Wadsworth, 2006
Second Edition, 2012
Aesthetics: A Comprehensive Anthology
(with Aaron Meskin)
Blackwell, 2008
Second Edition (with Stephanie A. Ross and Sandra Shapshay), 2018.
Happiness: Classic and Contemporary Readings
(with Christine Vitrano)
Oxford University Press, 2008
The Meaning of Life, 3rd Edition: A Reader
(with E. M. Klemke)
Oxford University Press, 2008
Fourth Edition, 2018

Seven Masterpieces of Philosophy
>   Pearson Longman, 2008

The Elements of Philosophy: Readings From Past and Present
>   (with Tamar Szabó Gendler and Susanna Siegel)
>   Oxford University Press, 2008

Exploring Philosophy of Religion: An Introductory Anthology
>   Oxford University Press, 2009
>   Second Edition, 2016

Exploring Ethics: An Introductory Anthology
>   Oxford University Press, 2009
>   Second Edition, 2011
>   Third Edition, 2014
>   Fourth Edition, 2017

Philosophy of Education: The Essential Texts
>   Routledge, 2009

Political Problems
>   (with Robert B. Talisse)
>   Prentice Hall, 2011

Thinking About Logic: Classic Essays
>   (with Robert B. Talisse and Scott F. Aikin)
>   Westview Press, 2011

Fate, Time, and Language: An Essay on Free Will by David Foster Wallace
>   (with Maureen Eckert)
>   Columbia University Press, 2011

Moral Problems in Higher Education
>   Temple University Press, 2011

Political Philosophy in the Twenty-First Century
>   (with Robert B. Talisse)
>   Westview Press, 2013

Portraits of American Philosophy
>   Rowman & Littlefield, 2013

Reason and Religions: Philosophy Looks at the World's Religious Beliefs
>   Wadsworth/Cengage Learning, 2014

Freedom and the Self: Essays on the Philosophy of David Foster Wallace
>   (with Maureen Eckert)
>   Columbia University Press, 2015

The World of Philosophy
>   Oxford University Press, 2016
>   Second Edition, 2019

Principles of Moral Philosophy: Classic and Contemporary Approaches
  (with Andrew T. Forcehimes)
  Oxford University Press, 2017
Foundations of Moral Philosophy: Readings in Metaethics
  (with Andrew T. Forcehimes)
  Oxford University Press, 2017
Exploring Moral Problems: An Introductory Anthology
  (with Andrew T. Forcehimes)
  Oxford University Press, 2018
Philosophers in the Classroom: Essays on Teaching
  (with Alexandra Bradner and Andrew Mills)
  Hackett Publishing Company, 2018

Index

Made in the USA
Middletown, DE
05 June 2021

41159021R00064